ROVER, GET OFF HER LEG!

To June
Hopefully you can find
some tricks in here that will work!
for Deckands and the foster dogs.
Best wishes,
Darlene Ard...

ROVER,
GET OFF
HER LEG!

Pet Etiquette for the Dog Who
Pees on Your Rug, Steals the Roast, and
Poops in Improper Places

DARLENE ARDEN

Health Communications, Inc.
Deerfield Beach, Florida

www.hcibooks.com

DISCLAIMER: The information in this book does not replace a consultation with a certified animal behaviorist, veterinarian, or other qualified animal professional.

Library of Congress Cataloging-in-Publication Data

Arden, Darlene.
    Rover, get off her leg : pet etiquette for the dog who pees on your rug, steals the roast, and poops in improper places / Darlene Arden.
        p. cm.
    Includes bibliographical references.
    ISBN-13: 978-0-7573-0544-3 (trade paper)
    ISBN-10: 0-7573-0544-X (trade paper)
    1. Dogs—Behavior. 2. Dogs—Training. I. Title.
SF433.A73 2007
636.7'0887—dc22

                                                        2007008968

Publisher: Health Communications, Inc.
            3201 S.W. 15th Street
            Deerfield Beach, FL 33442-8190

Interior design and formatting by Lawna Patterson Oldfield
Interior illustrations by Mary Jhung

ALWAYS FOR MY
MOTHER

CONTENTS

ACKNOWLEDGMENTS

I wouldn't have had the opportunity to write this rather unique behavior book had it not been for Michele Matrisciani, editorial director at Health Communications, Inc. She entrusted me with this project, not just for my expertise as a dog writer and a behavior consultant but because she knew it would require a warped sense of humor to reach the dog owners who are convinced they are alone in their attempt to cope with various dog behaviors. She was barking up the right tree.

I want to thank my editor, Allison Janse, and the team at HCI.

I'm grateful to those who shared their stories, no matter how embarrassing (most of the names in this book were changed to protect the "guilty"), so that the readers might understand that they are not alone. It's a wonderful thing when you can laugh at your problems and understand that there is help available, that the situation isn't hopeless, and that others have been where you are and have survived.

I'm thankful to every dog who has walked into my life, whether mine or someone else's. Each has taught me something. I've learned from them and loved them all.

Last, but never least, I want to thank my chosen family, especially my chosen sisters from around the United States and around the world. You have always been supportive, and I am both very lucky and very thankful to have such a special group of women in my life.

INTRODUCTION

As a certified animal behavior consultant, I've heard all the dog-related horror stories:

- "When I walk my dog, he practically pulls my arm out of the socket if he sees another dog. How can I get him to walk nicely . . . or at least keep him from dragging me down the street?"

- "My dog seems to have selective hearing; he will tear through the house when he hears me open a bag of chips but won't budge when I call him to come."

- "I don't want to have dinner parties anymore because my dog is always being a pest under the table. I don't blame my friends for wanting to avoid her pleading eyes. Please help me get my human social life back!"

For years, owners of dogs of every temperament and breed have tracked me down to help resolve these kinds of problems. Believe me, as someone who has spent nearly my entire life with dogs—personally, professionally, and as a doggie mom myself—I understand their frustration. The day you bring your new puppy or dog home, you find you need some help, just like clueless parents who buy *What to Expect When You're Expecting*. Just like kids, dogs come with their own set of behaviors and preferences. Once you start talking about your dog with other owners, you're going to find out how much you have in common. Most of us have slept in uncomfortable positions so the dog has enough room to sleep on the bed, or we've fallen asleep to the snoring of a dog curled up on the pillow next to us. Having a dog should be fun, and it can be. But there's no such thing as an instant companion, and there's no simple recipe: just add water and stir.

I understand the potential pitfalls. You want to know what to do when your dog barks all day and your neighbors are sending you nasty notes or dirty looks. Or what to do if your dog gets expelled from doggie daycare for growling at another four-legged kid. To quote a former U.S. president, "I feel your pain." I can't go door to door, though, which is why I've written this book.

The adorable, mischievous puppy who has you at your wit's end can become the dog of your dreams with a little time, patience, and love. This book can help guide you through the challenging times and, with any luck, make you laugh as you realize that others have gone through the same thing . . . or worse.

Dogs do all sorts of things that we, as humans, don't find acceptable, especially in public, like humping, peeing in the wrong places, and stealing food. Your dog isn't doing any of this to spite you. Really, he isn't. He just needs training in the basics of canine comportment to live peaceably in the world of humans. Consider this your pocket guide to an (almost) perfectly politically correct pet.

Will he still embarrass you from time to time? Sure! Stuff happens. To make you feel a little better about your own "parenting ability," I've included stories from other dog owners about their embarrassing moments and their dogs' over-the-top behaviors. In nearly all cases, I've changed the names to protect the "guilty," but the stories are true.

Throughout the book, you'll also notice "Top 10" icons. These Top 10 most annoying behaviors are the most frequent complaints I've heard time and time again from frazzled dog owners and professionals who work with dogs. While some of them are relatively harmless behaviors, albeit embarrassing, others are more serious offenses. If you can solve even half of these issues, you'll be on your way to a great life with your furry friend—and you might even keep some of your human friends while you and your dog are at it.

Nearly everything can be fixed, and every relationship can be better and more fun, even the best of them.

PART 1

BASIC TRAINING 101

DOGS ARE AMAZING CREATURES AND

wonderful friends. We know that they're living, breathing, sentient beings, but sometimes people forget that they view the world differently than the way we do. This is because, for them, it *is* a little different.

In all the years I've owned dogs, been around other people's dogs, and helped owners with behavior problems, I've learned that "behavior problems" are not always what they seem to be. For example, a dog who refuses to go outside one day isn't being obstinate just to aggravate his owner. It's up to the owner to think of what occurred the previous day that may have frightened the dog, causing him to feel more secure indoors. It may not have meant anything to the owner that the wind picked up a tarp as the dog walked past it, but to the dog, it was a frightening experience that he'd just as soon not repeat.

Because we love our dogs as much as—if not more than—some humans, sometimes we forget that we're living with another species, so we anthropomorphize, or explain away the behavior in human terms. Here's a perfect example: I had been invited to the home of a distant cousin for the first time while on a business trip. Not long after I walked in the door, his Toy Poodle latched on to my leg and began humping rather enthusiastically. Apparently, he and his wife had never attempted to change the dog's behavior. Maybe they thought it was perfectly acceptable. Distant cousin and his wife merely exclaimed, "Oh! He likes you!" Uh, not exactly, and just for the record: I don't date out of my species! By laughing at the humper's behavior, the owners unknowingly created and no doubt perpetuated a bad habit with every unsuspecting person who had the "pleasure" of walking through their door.

We want dogs to fit well into our households, and it's our responsibility to understand them and to teach them what to do in place of a behavior that's unwanted by human standards. How do you do this? You begin with proper training and socialization. A few words before you start: the most important thing your dog needs when you train him (besides patience) is consistency. So, before you begin any type of training, make sure that you and all of your family members are on the same page. "If Mom says no, ask Grandma," may be funny when talking about human children, but it will confuse your canine family member and undermine your training efforts.

Consistently Inconsistent

"While teaching training classes for our local kennel club, a woman came in for class with an elderly Toy Poodle. She explained that the dog would bite her whenever she picked him up. Because the problem didn't appear to be physical with the dog, but rather behavioral between the two of them, I suggested a solution and sent her home. At next week's class, the woman said the behavior was still occurring. I asked if she was following my suggestion *every* time the dog would bite at her. The woman looked at me with surprise and said, 'You mean I have to do this more than once?' I explained that as an acquired behavior (a 'bad habit,' as it were), it may reasonably take some time to unlearn. I only then thought to ask how long this particular habit had been in place. The woman replied, 'Fifteen years.' " —Ted

Please let me say it again: When you begin any type of training, consistency is key.

With so many different training methods out there—doggie boot camps, doggie whisperers, and others, how do you know which one is right for your dog?

Operant Conditioning Is Optimal

Some people swear that their dogs have "selective hearing." The dog won't listen, can't listen, or doesn't listen. The real answers are either that the owner hasn't really tried or, more important, has tried a method that the dog won't respond to. And only too often the dog is far more intelligent than the owner realizes.

The Dog Who Never Listens

"My husband gets very upset with my dear old Staffordshire Terrier, Lolly, because she doesn't respond to him. She's my girl. She never does anything wrong, and she never really does anything right, because basically—she just doesn't *do* anything! We always joke that when doG was handing out the brains, Lolly thought he said trains and missed hers. You know, the light-is-on-but-nobody-is-home type of dog?

One day, we went to purchase some meat from the butcher shop. Lolly always rides in the back of my car and has never touched anything that doesn't belong to her. I've put BBQ chicken, dog meat, and all other kinds of yummies back there with her and she's not even so much as sniffed. During this particular outing my husband put the meat in the car, and said, 'Here you go, Lolly, have a T-bone.' So, she did. Just *one* T-bone. She carefully unwrapped the meat, took one T-bone, and left the other three on the polystyrene tray, covered in plastic. My husband got really grumpy with her, but when I explained what he'd done, he started to laugh. Maybe Lolly finally did listen to him, and maybe she isn't that dumb after all. **"** —Annie

That would certainly be my take on it. Research has shown that dogs can count up to three. Beyond that, if a dog can count, he's considered a doggy genius. No matter how many kisses I gave one of my dogs, he would give me the same number in return. I always varied the number and there was no pattern to it, no rhyme or reason, yet he was always accurate in returning the same number of kisses. That was the same dog who was told he could bring two toys whenever we traveled. He would carefully select two from the many toys he owned and drop each one into the open suitcase. Sometimes, smart and foolish can go hand in . . . er . . . paw.

Never underestimate your dog's intelligence.

In my years of experience, I've come to rely on *operant conditioning* (commonly called *clicker training*), with *lure-and-reward training* as my second choice. Both are discussed in the following sections.

For anyone who slept through Psych 101, operant conditioning dates back to the 1930s and the famed psychologist B. F. Skinner. The dog, in this case, is *operant,* choosing what he wants to do because he learns quickly that he will be rewarded for it. This type of training is positive and empowering because it gives the dog the opportunity to think and to respond.

Any training you do should be gentle and positive. There is no punishment involved with clicker or lure-and-reward training methods. While punishment-based training may or may not work in the short term, in the long term, there will be problems. If you coerce the dog to do something based on fear, he may do it at the time, but may respond quite differently later on. You will see far better results if you train your dog with love and positive reinforcement instead of fear and punishment. And you'll have more fun doing it.

Clicker Training

Clickers break through the human/canine language barrier because they are more consistent than the human voice, allowing the dog to understand exactly what you want. Clicker trainers often talk about the *lightbulb* or *aha! moment* when they see in the dog's eyes that he has made the connection and understands what you want. When clicker training, the *treat*—whatever your dog likes best—is his payment for doing his job well. Because clicker training teaches the dog to problem solve by figuring out what you want, it's fun for the dog, and because he's trying to get you to "click," he thinks he's training you! Clicker training works without any punishment; the sessions are fun and require only a couple of minutes of training each day.

Lure-and-Reward Training

Lure-and-reward training is a little different from clicker training and is useful for anyone with a physical handicap that will not allow for a quick response with a clicker. With lure-and-reward, if you want the dog to sit, you lure him into position by taking a training treat and slowly moving it up over his head, yet close enough for him to see. As his head comes up, his butt will automatically hit the floor, and you can praise him and deliver the treat. It's a very rapid way to teach a dog to sit and learn basic behaviors, but for more complex behaviors, clicker training is a better choice. You can pretty easily "chain" behaviors by breaking down the complex behavior into smaller parts and rewarding for them, eventually putting them all together.

Training Questions to Ask Your Breeder

If you've gotten a puppy from a reputable breeder, it's possible she will have started training before you bring home your new family member. The breeder may have taught all the puppies to sit politely before their food dishes were put down on the floor. Some of the more progressive breeders begin clicker training while the puppies are still in the whelping box and may even teach their puppies tricks like shaking hands or playing a child's toy piano. No, you're not going to get a concert pianist, but you're going to get a bright dog who enjoys doing things and who has begun the training process. He has learned how to learn. Ask the breeder to show you what the puppy knows so that you can keep doing it to reinforce the desired behaviors.

Winning by Default

When beginning operant training, the very first thing that you teach your dog will become his *default behavior*— that is, what he will do in situations when he doesn't know what to do. This means that before you start your first training session, you have to make a decision: do you want your dog to always sit, lie down, or settle in a special place when he doesn't know what to do? Show dogs are taught to stand first so that they will always stand nicely in the conformation ring. For dogs who aren't going into the show ring, the best thing to teach as the default behavior is either the Sit or Down behaviors. Sit is easier to teach, so you may want to start with that.

After you've decided on a default behavior, you'll need to choose a clicker. If your dog is sound-sensitive, you can purchase a clicker that makes a softer sound, or you can wrap your clicker with tape and keep it in your pocket while you train. To find a wide assortment of clickers and other equipment, go to www.clickertraining.com, a resource created by Karen Pryor, the internationally recognized pioneer of clicker training whose books are widely read. Another excellent source is www.legacycanine.com, the website of respected dog trainer and author Terry Ryan, who invented the Click Stick, a target stick and clicker all in one. A target stick for those who are not yet familiar with one is a wonderful training tool. You can use a dowel, a folding target stick, or a Click Stick. You teach the dog to touch the tip of it with his nose. Once he understands that, you can use that tip of the stick to point toward where you want him to go or what you want him to touch. That is called targeting. It's a wonderful help while training any dog and is especially useful if you are tall, have a small dog, and don't want to keep bending over. Also, rather than have the dog strain to look up at you, you can train him to target somewhere in the vicinity of your calf while teaching him to walk politely beside you. You can also pat your leg as you walk, keeping his attention by talking and giving treats when he's paying attention. If he pulls, stop walking. Say his name and start walking again.

Next you'll need some tiny training treats (itty-bitty pieces of chicken or turkey or cheese will do) and have them in a dish near your hand. Be sure to figure all treats into your dog's daily ration of food because you don't want him to pack on the pounds as you train. Load or *charge* the clicker by clicking and treating your dog in rapid succession about half a dozen times. Now your dog understands that click means treat. The click is an *event marker,* telling your dog what he has done right. Keep in mind that the treat doesn't have to be food. Some dogs like a bit of play with a favorite toy, while others like a pat. Once you discover what treat your dog likes best, keep the treat consistent.

Teaching Your Dog to Sit

Most people choose Sit as their dog's default behavior. All dogs have to sit sooner or later, so you click when his butt hits the floor and give him a little treat. If you are impatient (not a good training tool; you really need patience and consistency to train a dog!), you can lure the dog into a Sit by taking the treat and moving it slowly up in front of him and up over his head. As his head goes back to follow your hand, his butt will automatically go down. Click and treat. But fade that lure out fast, just as quickly as the dog begins to respond (so fade it out with just a few repetitions) or training will take longer.

Important note to overly chatty owners: don't say a word until the dog has done the behavior correctly about half a dozen times, and then you can add the word "Sit!" Be sure he knows what you want before you give him a name for the behavior. Always end each training session on a positive note when your dog has done something correctly; then you can click and give him a *jackpot,* which is several treats at one time. Then tell him the game is over. A few short training sessions each day will be fun for both of you and will help your dog learn quite quickly. Practice all behaviors in several rooms so that your pup doesn't think that he only does it in one special place.

The Impatient Owner

66We took our adopted one-year-old dog to an outdoor mall to socialize him and to practice some basic commands. As passersby cooed and 'awwed' at our cute dog, I was trying to be patient as our dog stood there, not responding to me. By the fifth or sixth 'Sit!' I found my crescendo rising with my blood pressure. Why won't he just sit? I lost my sensitive training voice and morphed into

Mommy Dearest, yelling out, 'Sit!' Just then he squatted and proceeded to shi* right there on the sidewalk, much to everyone's amusement. My husband said, 'Oh, he heard you all right! He was telling you just what he thought of your losing your cool.'" —Leslie

Yes, dogs are masters at responding to our body language and to our tone of voice. This is why, when training, you should never say a cue word more than once. You simply say one "Sit" without raising your voice. If your dog doesn't respond, ignore him. Don't repeat, "Sit! Sit! Sit!" The more upset you sound, the more upset your dog will be. In Leslie's situation, the dog was simply confused, distracted by his surroundings, and needed more practice. In the event that a training session goes badly, have your dog do something simple so you can praise him and give him a treat, so that the negative experience isn't the thing that stays in his mind.

WHAT NOT TO DO DURING TRAINING: Throw the choke, electronic, and prong collars away because these can do more harm than good. You also don't need to use a gruff voice as some people suggest. Your dog's hearing is much more acute than ours. Since they are very good at reading body language, dogs will understand more from your body language and a quiet voice than by yelling, which will only frighten them. Your training mantra should be, "Ignore bad behavior, reward good behavior." It's easy to remember. Take a deep breath and relax.

Other Essential Behaviors
Every Dog Should Know

In addition to learning the Sit behavior, your dog should be able to display the following essential behaviors: Come, Lie Down, Stay, Drop It, and Leave It. These are all considered essential behaviors because they can save your dog's life. Think about the various circumstances when your dog would need to know some of these things. Come is incredibly important, and your dog must come every time. If he's gotten away from you and is about to run across the road into oncoming traffic, Come, Sit, or Stay will be invaluable in keeping him out of harm's way. Drop It can get him to drop something out of his mouth that could be harmful in one way or another (a sharp object, a poisonous frog or plant, and so on). Better yet, Leave It can stop him from picking up that object in the first place.

Teaching Your Dog to Come

Because teaching your dog to come can save his life, you need to teach that behavior early on in your relationship. In fact, start working on it within a day of bringing him home. If you have an older dog or an adopted dog, treat him just like a new puppy and teach him the very same way. If your dog is deaf, you can train using a flashlight. There are always ways to train around special needs. Operant conditioning is a wonderful tool and will motivate any dog once he learns to "play the game," because that's what it seems like to him. Never give up just because you have an older dog, and certainly don't give up on an adopted dog. These dogs need you and want to bond with you. Training is another way to help them bond, and it's especially important for all dogs to know that when they come to you, something good will always happen.

WHAT TO DO WHEN TEACHING YOUR DOG TO

COME: Clicker training is a very easy way to teach your dog to come. First, teach your dog that click means treat by using tiny bits of chicken or turkey or even pieces of his kibble. Click and treat at least half a dozen times in a row. Have each member of your family sit in a different place or in a different room of your choice, with each person taking turns calling your dog by name in a happy voice. Don't do it in any particular order; just be sure that everyone does it. When he comes, click and give him a treat. Praise him lavishly. And always end the session on a happy note, with a few extra treats given at one time (the jackpot). You have to practice this for only a few minutes a couple of times each day. He'll soon learn to respond happily to his name.

WHAT TO DO WHEN YOUR DOG WON'T COME:

If your dog runs away from you and will not come, get another person who can circle around and get him from the other side of the street, yard, or wherever. If calling him in a happy voice isn't working, sit down and pretend to cry. If your dog is bonded to you, he will come to see what's wrong. (You'll probably feel like crying anyway, so it won't be that difficult.) If your dog has run off, borrow a Havahart trap from a local Humane Society and put his favorite food in it. If he has truly disappeared, you'll need to alert every veterinary office and dog officer in nearby towns and display flyers that offer a reward everywhere.

Be sure your dog or puppy has a collar and tag and is microchipped. That microchip, which must be registered, can not only reunite you with your lost pet but can also prove identification.

Teaching Your Dog to Trade You or Drop It

To teach your dog to trade an off-limits item, you need to have ready an item that he values as even or better. Wait until he's playing with a toy. Walk over to him with a new toy in hand and show great interest in it. When he, too, begins to show interest and begins to reach for the new toy, click and give the new toy to him or simply say, "Trade You." (If you're using clicker training, the words always come after the dog has mastered the new behavior.) It's a game, and he thinks he's winning. Ah ha! You both win! You can teach him to drop something by saying, "Drop it!" and rewarding him when he complies.

Trade You, Fibber

❝Just about everyone in Labrador Land knows about Fibber, better known to his friends and admirers as Fat Rotten Fibber, from Laura Dedering's Folklaur Labradors in New Jersey. Fibber was a Black show male out of the Number-One Lab in the United States at the time, a champion in both the United States and Canada with an Obedience title as well. Although Fibber didn't work out as a show dog, he was my first Lab who made quite an impression on everyone he encountered.

We had moved from New Jersey to North Carolina, and I was the show chairman of the Raleigh-Durham Labrador Retriever Club's first independent specialty, a dog show in which only one breed is shown. We had invited the very well-known judge Jane Palmer of Jayncourt Labradors to judge our show. After the show, she came to my home to have dinner before returning to the United Kingdom.

We were sitting eating dinner and everyone was enjoying themselves when, lo and behold, in the middle of the meal, who comes prancing into the dining room with Jane's purse proudly hanging out of his mouth, but Fibber. Of course, I was mortified. Jane was very nice and calm and asked Fibber to give her the purse, which—thank God!—he did. But I thought I would like to just crawl under the table and die. I had visions of Jane going back to England and telling all the other breeders about that awful dog, Fibber, who steals purses when you visit her home.

Much to my mortification, Jane did tell several other breeders about Fibber, and several have remarked when they visited me that they would make sure they held tightly to their purses when they came for dinner. " —Evie

Because Fibber was so good about returning the purse, it would be tempting to pass it off as a parlor trick. Fibber's owner was correct in remaining calm and not chasing the dog in an attempt to retrieve the purse. That would only have made Fibber think she was up for a game of chase. In situations like these, you'll find it much more effective to use the Trade You or Drop It behaviors instead.

Teaching Your Dog to Leave It

Because dogs are closer to the ground than you are and are naturally curious, they seem to always find interesting things. Those things can range from embarrassing to downright dangerous. When this happens, and your dog spots something on the pavement or in your home, tell him to look at you or ask him for another behavior like Sit. Be creative! If he has already picked the item up, have a treat ready and say, "Leave It," and take the forbidden thing away.

The Treasure-Hunter

"I was invited to evaluate a litter of Italian Greyhound puppies at the upscale home of a well-to-do woman I had met only once before. As I usually did, I took along my first champion, Pagliacci. I loved to show him off—especially how well-behaved he was. All told, there was my friend Pat, the owner of the stud, the litter owner, two of her non-doggie friends, and me. We were all engrossed in looking at the week-old litter and trying to determine how they could all turn out black when the sire and dam were both fawn with no known black behind them. (We later learned that the actual sire of the litter was the breeder's Champion Black Miniature Poodle and not my friend's Italian Greyhound.) It suddenly occurred to me that Pagliacci, who had been in a Down Stay, was no longer in the room. I called him, and shortly, he came trotting in, proudly displaying the prize he held between his teeth—an intact and obviously well-used sanitary napkin.

> The moral of this story: If you have dogs, dispose of potentially embarrassing items very carefully. Also, don't assume that an obedience-trained dog won't ever make you blush. " —Melanie

Melanie is right. Never assume anything because, chances are, you'll live to regret it. If your dog is the one who has found the "treasure," apologize. Don't forget to tell your dog to Drop It and Leave It. Always have some sort of treat or a toy with you so that you can reward him for responding. One more thing: clean up before company arrives. I don't mean the usual straightening. I mean that if there's anything you don't want company to see, be certain it's in a place where no dog can reach it!

Teaching Your Dog to Lie Down

Training your dog to lie down is easy with a clicker. When your puppy or dog lies down, click and treat. It's easier if you capture this behavior in a small room where there will be few distractions. Also, do it with the door closed so your dog or puppy can't go wandering off in search of something more fascinating. Another way to do this is to go about your business—listen to music or read a newspaper—but as soon as he settles down, click and treat immediately. Because your dog will probably be clicker-wise by this time, you're going to have to ignore the other behaviors he's going to throw at you that have already worked to get him a treat. When he lies down again, click and treat. He'll soon catch on. Repeat this about half a dozen times or so, and then end the session with a jackpot.

Teaching Your Dog to Stay

Stay is an important behavior for your dog to learn. After your dog has learned Down, he can learn Stay if you back away from him a bit, click, and say, "Good!" in a happy tone of voice when he doesn't move. Deliver the treat. Do this in slow stages by taking a few steps backward at a time, backing farther away with each session.

Be patient. Every dog learns at his own pace. But it's never too late to learn, even if it takes an older dog a little longer. With clicker training, even older dogs will surprise you and learn more rapidly than you ever expected.

Is My Older Dog Rebelling?

With dogs, the "teenage years" can occur anywhere from four or six months to two years, depending on the breed, but most commonly they begin at six or seven months. During this time, your dog may behave as if he has forgotten everything he ever learned, no matter if you use clicker or lure and reward or anything else. This is a normal stage, just as it is in human children when they begin to push boundaries and forget they ever learned anything you've taught them. Keep him interested by teaching him new things to do, and you'll eventually have your wonderful dog back. It may take a few weeks, but stick with short, fun training sessions and keep them varied, throwing in some of the basic commands every so often.

Your Doggie's Social Circuit

One of the most important things you can do for your puppy or dog is to properly socialize him. The window of opportunity for socialization comes within the first twelve weeks. In other words, you have a limited time in which to make an impact. For every day past those twelve weeks, socialization becomes more difficult (but not impossible, which is why it is so important to begin at any time and continue throughout his lifetime). Lack of socialization can lead to fear aggression, which is the worst form of aggression, no matter what size the dog.

Was Your Dog Bred to Be Social?

Proper socialization starts with a responsible breeder. From the first day of life, the puppy should be gently picked up and put down. This is the neonate's introduction to humans—how they feel and how they smell, since those little eyes aren't open yet. As the puppies grow, they must have time with Mom and littermates, who will teach them to speak "dog," learning all the body language that will help them throughout their lives when they encounter other dogs.

As the puppies begin to grow, within a few weeks they should be spending their days in an exercise pen in the breeder's kitchen or den, where they're exposed to all the sights, smells, and sounds of a busy household. People coming through should not be allowed to touch the pups until they have washed their hands, and they should take off their shoes before entering the room, especially before the puppies have had their first vaccinations. They're protected by Mom's vaccinations while tiny, gaining that protection through colostrum, the first milk they nurse from Mom. But that protection wears off and they must have vaccinations of their own to prevent life-threatening illnesses.

WHAT TO DO WHEN SOCIALIZING YOUR DOG:

Your dog should meet people of every possible description, size, shape, and color—people wearing hats, people with eyeglasses, people with beards, and whatever else you can think of to be sure he's socialized to everyone and everything. Take him to a strip mall to walk him, and be sure to supervise his encounters with people so the experiences are always good. Riding in the car will be fun if he knows that he

has happy experiences when he goes for rides. Let him walk
with you in the city to see and hear buses, airplanes, and trains,
as well as in the quieter countryside. He should be accustomed
to all sorts of sights and sounds. There's nothing better than a
well-socialized dog, a companion you don't have to leave at
home or lock in another room when company arrives.

Dogs and Children

All interactions between dogs and children should be
carefully supervised. Make sure children touch your dog
gently. Always have them sit on the floor when patting
puppies, and don't let them pick the puppies up. This way,
there's no chance they'll accidentally drop or otherwise
injure them. Some dogs will simply walk away from a child
who is becoming a pest, but not always. It's up to you to
protect both the puppy and the child. This is, without a
shadow of a doubt, your responsibility.

 WHAT NOT TO DO WHEN SOCIALIZING YOR DOG:
Don't leave your dog at home all the time, only
taking him to the veterinarian or the groomer. How
can you expect him to enjoy a ride in the car if the only times

he's in one is to go somewhere to be prodded, poked, bathed, combed, brushed, and so on? Sure, you can tell him he's going with you on vacation and talk about the beach or the lake until you're blue in the face. But if he hasn't experienced it, he won't understand that good things happen to good dogs when they go in the car. Also, don't yell at him because he won't get in the car. And don't coddle him and call him your "widdle baby-cakes," or he's going to think everything is a monster from which only you can protect him.

Don't flood your puppy or adopted dog with too many experiences at once. Go slowly. You have a lifetime together, and you don't want to frighten him. He's learning, whether he's a new pup coming into your home, an older rescue dog, or a dog you've raised all or most of his life. The process will still be the same. The main difference is that the rescue dog will probably come with baggage, and I don't mean a suitcase full of toys. I mean problems, especially if he has been abused. This makes it even more important for you to be patient, consistent, and loving.

Socialization is very important, but don't do it all at once! Flooding any dog—but especially a rescue dog—with too many new experiences at once will only confuse and frighten him, and that's exactly what you don't want to do. Adopting an older dog or taking in a rescue is giving that dog a new lease on life, and these dogs seem so much more grateful to have a loving home.

No matter how old your dog is or when you got him, he may have behavior problems. The point of this book is to help you avoid them or resolve those already in place. With your older or adopted dog, go back to what you would have done if he were a puppy and start there. For example, things like housetraining take less time with an older dog since he has adult kidneys and can "hold it" longer than a puppy. You can do a wonderful job of socializing an older dog if you remember, just as with the new pup, not to flood him with too many experiences at once. He, too, is just learning about life in your household.

The Partying Pup

" While in seminary, one of our professors invited several of us to a private Christmas party at his home. He had a doctorate of divinity and was the pastor of one of the largest churches in the Washington, D.C., area. We all felt honored that we had been invited to his home.

The evening of the party, the group of us arrived on time, and our professor greeted us at the front door. As we entered the house, his absolutely beautiful Golden Retriever entered with us and bounded up the stairs into the living room, making himself comfortable on the couch. A few other guests had arrived before us, and they began petting the big Golden. Knowing that I was a 'dog person,' the professor asked me whether I thought the dog was a good example of a Golden. Fortunately, he was, as I would have been hard pressed to critique this esteemed man's dog. Needless to say, the dog had become the center of attention. He settled in and occupied the greater part of the living room couch, enjoying the attention and strokes.

A few minutes later, my professor asked me for the dog's name. Huh? 'I thought he was your dog,' I said. 'My dog?' asked the professor. 'I assumed he was your dog and that you had brought him with you to the party.' I told him that I had never seen the dog before and that he had just entered the house with us from the front yard. We all laughed as one of the guests escorted the dog to the front door.

It turned out that the dog was new to the neighborhood, and upon exiting, the dog's escort spotted the owner walking down the block calling, 'Rex!' Owner located, dog fed snacks, party-goers had a good laugh. " —Lynne

The Dos and Don'ts of Doggie Playdates

To get your dog used to being around other dogs, you can take him to a dog park or arrange a playdate with another dog of the same size and age, one that you know is friendly.

Let dogs meet each other on canine terms: allow them to sniff each other and to play together. Because you don't want them fighting over toys or bones, you're really better off without such items. However, if you do bring a toy, bring one for each dog. Do not, however, bring a toy to a dog park because a toy can set off a resource-guarding fight.

Only bring a toy to privately arranged playdates with a friend, and be sure everyone is supervising very carefully. Although most dogs love to run and tussle together, make sure rough-and-tumble play is confined to dogs of the same size. Even though they may be the same age, a smaller canine can be injured, even accidentally, by a larger one. Supervise the play, and be sure that one dog isn't bullying the other. You may hear lots of growls that sound vicious. Most people mistake these play sounds for genuine problems. They're not. The dogs are play-fighting.

Watch their body language carefully to see that your dog is relaxed. If you want to know if your dog is stressed, look for such body language as lip licking, head turning, yawning when he's not tired, or licking his feet incessantly. If your dog runs away from a group of dogs, he's telling you that he's stressed and needs to relax. Keep him away from the other dogs and help him relax by first relaxing yourself. Remember that your dog is reading your body language every minute. While you're trying to relax, suck on a mint because that will mask any signs of your stressed body chemistry. The dog's nose knows!

Watch to see any danger signs that the play is becoming more aggressive. If one dog is aggressive or a bully, try to distract them from each other before you find yourself in the dangerous position of trying to break up a dog fight. It's always best to scope out a dog park in advance without your dog. Watch to see who is there and how well they supervise their dogs. Go at different times and different days to see who shows up when and which group will best suit you and your dog.

Now you should have the basics of training and socialization down. You and your dog are ready to tackle specific problem behaviors that are explained in the next chapters.

PART 2

PLUMBING PROBLEMS

DOG PEOPLE HAVE THEIR OWN IDEA

about what makes for interesting conversation. I'll never forget traveling with a large group of dog people to a dog show in Bermuda. Most of us were staying at the same hotel, so nearly every table in the dining room was occupied by dog people who thought nothing of having a discussion during dinner about dog food and its . . . er . . . end result. It's somewhat embarrassing to think later how the non-doggy diners reacted to the discussion surrounding them as it became livelier and more descriptive with nearly everyone participating.

Housetraining How-Tos

Conversation is one thing, but getting down to the inevitable dog/owner problem of how to handle the bathroom situation can be quite another. Like many human parents who worry that their slow-to-learn children might still be wearing diapers in college, nothing causes more questions and stress than trying to train a dog to "go." Housetraining starts the minute your puppy or dog arrives at her new home (reputable breeders start before then). Take her to a preselected sheltered spot before you bring her into the house and give her a chance to relieve herself. This requires consistency and patience.

 WHAT TO DO DURING HOUSETRAINING: Find one spot where you will always take your puppy or dog to go. Try to find a secluded place; after all, you wouldn't really want to go outdoors with everyone watching, would you? This is especially true for female dogs, who have to squat and are vulnerable to attack in that position. Always use the same cue words to tell the dog what to do; that way she'll always know what's expected of her. You can say "Go potty," "Park it," or "Hurry, hurry!" Whatever you choose, stick with it! You can also reinforce it further, if necessary, by using a clicker as added incentive to understand that she is doing what you want, where you want her to do it.

Give her a cue as you get ready to go out. Get her harness or flat buckle collar and leash and say, "Let's go!" When you get her to her special place, you can tell her whatever word or phrase you have chosen. Take a high-value treat with you, a tiny bit of something the dog or puppy gets at no other time—something really special. As soon as her feet hit the ground and she assumes the position, praise her, sounding really excited. And when she's done, give her the treat and tell her that she's a genius. You can phase out the treat once she's reliably trained enough to ask you to take her out by running to the door or just looking at you with a particularly meaningful expression. (This is why learning to read your dog's body language is important.)

When housetraining, sleep in sweats or scrubs and keep your shoes handy because you'll have to take your dog out in the middle of the night if she has to go. If you don't take her out and she makes a mistake, it's your fault, not hers. If you have a puppy, you'll have to go out more frequently—after she eats, after she plays, before bedtime, and when she first gets up in the morning—because puppies can't hold it for very long. If you have an older dog in the house, she'll help train the newcomer because observational learning is a many-splendored thing. Be patient: training takes time. In fact, small dogs usually take a full year before they're reliably housetrained, while larger dogs can be reliably trained in a month or two, depending upon her age and how developed her kidneys and her ability to wait longer periods of time are. If you've acquired an older dog who was trained before, it can take as little as a week to adjust the dog to your home and schedule. However, it can take anywhere from a couple of days to a month for an adult dog who was not previously housetrained. That, of course, is just a "guess-timate." All dogs are individuals, so just let it happen, and don't telegraph your anxiety to the dog.

 ## WHAT NOT TO DO WHEN HOUSETRAINING:

Don't yell at the dog, scream, or punish her in any way. Don't yank her collar or give her a leash pop. If you catch her in the middle of making a mess, use a verbal interrupter like "Uh!" or a simple sound to distract her. Everyone makes mistakes, and if you yell at your dog, you're not going to do anything good for your relationship. Dogs really don't remember that the mess is theirs because their memory of such events lasts mere seconds. Simply clean up any mess without saying anything, and then take her to her special spot.

Eventually, she'll make the association. And never, ever, ever call your dog or puppy to you to punish her, or she'll never want to go to you when you want her. That could endanger her life if you're calling her away from a bad situation.

A Wee Thing

"My son was in the early stages of potty training and would be very proud of himself when he didn't have an accident in his diaper. He came up to me one day and said that he had gone 'poopy.' I asked if he had an accident, and he replied, 'No,' with a grin. I was proud of him and asked, 'Did you potty in the toilet like a big boy?' He replied, 'No,' still grinning. I asked, 'Well, where did you go?' 'In the yard like Disco!' he said. I didn't have the heart to tell him that was not a good thing, so I made my husband explain it to him." —Leslie

Help for the Regressing Dog

My dog, who had been reliably housetrained for over three years, keeps having accidents in the house. Why is she doing this?

Dogs who have accidents after being housetrained may have a urinary tract infection. Before you assume that it's a behavior problem, take your dog to your veterinarian for a physical checkup just to be sure that there's no underlying organic problem. Even without an infection, however, your dog may decide to pee on your bed, your shoes, your pillow, and so on. Why? That question can be answered only by what preceded the action. Write down any recent changes in your household. Has someone moved in or out? Has the dog's routine been upset? Has the dog been punished for something? Is she insecure for some reason? Some little dogs might feel afraid and want to surround themselves with their own smell in order to feel safer. If your dog is peeing in an inappropriate place, be sure to clean that place with a special odor remover that breaks down enzymes. These are available at pet-supply stores.

 WHAT TO DO WHEN YOUR DOG ISN'T HOUSE-TRAINED: If your dog isn't housetrained and you're afraid to leave her unsupervised, there are products to help. You can get a smaller dog a Belly Band—a canine version of a diaper. For larger dogs, you can improvise and use a child's soak-proof diaper, cutting out a hole in it for her tail.

And while we're on the subject of diapers, here's another potential clean-up problem: if you haven't spayed your female, she will go into season twice a year. This means that she will have a bloody discharge, which you won't appreciate on your furniture, bedding, etc. To avoid this, you can get Bitches Britches, the doggie version of a sanitary napkin and holder. You'll have to keep changing the sanitary napkin, of course. And won't that be fun? Not! But it's a helpful solution to a potential problem for some dogs.

If your dog isn't housetrained because you don't have time to walk her during the day, it's best to get someone to go to your house and walk her for you or enroll her in a good doggie daycare.

Choosing a Doggie Daycare

If you work full time, can't get home at lunchtime, or don't have anyone who can go in and give your dog some attention and exercise midday, you might want to consider enrolling your dog in doggie daycare. You'll have to do some investigation first, of course. Go without your dog. Look around. Is it clean? Are the dogs kept in safe conditions? Are they separated by size for playtime, and is that playtime supervised? (Just like little kids, there are bullies who have four legs. Someone has to be well aware of how the dogs relate to each other.) Are they using positive methods? Do they also take the dogs out for individual walks? Is there a nice area for rest periods? Each dog should have a separate place for naps.

Doggie daycare isn't cheap, but for the pet owner who works exceptionally long hours and wants to relax with his or her dog at night and not go out for long walks or runs during the week, this can be a good choice. One caveat: if someone offers to train your dog, think twice. In reality, it is the owner who is being trained, not the dog, so it doesn't do a whole lot of good if you're not there. If you choose this option, you'll have to learn the cues the dog knows and, most important, you'll want to know precisely how your dog is being trained because you want positive, not aversive, training.

Going to the Dogs

"When my daughter was two years old, I had three Dachshunds that I was trying to housetrain. I found one of those doggie litter pans at the local store and decided to try it out. Meanwhile, I was also trying to potty-train my daughter, so I was fairly busy. The dogs actually took to the litter box fairly easily and things were going well.

One day, I took my two-year-old daughter to my friend's house for a Tupperware party. Eleven of us women were all sitting in the living room chatting when my daughter walked in, dropped her drawers, and proceeded to poop in my friend's cat's litter box! After we all stopped gasping and picked our jaws up off the floor, my daughter proudly proclaimed, 'Doggies do it!' and marched off. It was, perhaps, my most embarrassing moment ever.

What's even funnier is that I had to go out and buy some of the disposable litter trays that sit down in the toilet to get my daughter to do her

> business in the right place! Can you imagine walk-
> ing into the Wal-Mart bathroom with your child
> and a litter box?! It finally worked, though. "
>
> —Tammy

 Who said dog owners couldn't be resourceful? Well, all's well that ends well, and everyone was house- and toilet-trained in the end.

Most Annoying Behavior: **The Anxious Urinator**

Anxious urination is a problem I hear about a lot, since dog owners don't want their guests to be greeted by a dog peeing in the entrance hall. *Anxious urination* happens when someone comes to the door, and the dog is so excited or anxious to see that person that she pees right there and then. It doesn't matter if the person is you coming home from work, a good friend, your minister, or a blind date. The dog is anxious. The dog pees.

WHAT ANXIOUS URINATION MEANS: Peeing isn't always quite as straightforward an event as the owner might think. As with most things dog-related, the owner's interpretation is strictly from human understanding, without considering the canine's point of view. Often, anxious urination is marking behavior: "Hey! This is *mine*!" Sometimes, they pee as a way to comfort themselves, by covering areas with their own smell. Occasionally, the motivation has to do with an interloper (in the dog's opinion) in her relationship with her owner; it may also be a sign of submission.

Love Is in the Air

66Shortly after I had graduated from college as a veterinary technician, my sister set me up on a blind date with her coworker's son, Ed. Ed phoned to invite me out to dinner, with only one request: I wear a dress. He insisted that all his dates wear dresses. Mind you, I was in my early twenties, extremely shy, considered Frisch's Big Boy to be fine dining, and owned one, maybe two, dresses.

But surely, as weird as it sounded, I could find a dress to wear.

Ed picked me up, met the family, and off we went to dinner at the Heavenly, an expensive, fancy restaurant where everyone, including the servers, were very snobbish and totally intimidating. Ed told me I could have anything I wanted, but he had to order it. (Okay, let's stroke that ego.) While we waited for our food, Ed asked if I'd mind if he asked my younger sister for a date. (Whew, at least I wouldn't be subjected to him again. Sibling rivalry can be a good thing!)

By the time we reached my house, it was storming, as in all great Shakespearean tragedies. When we opened the door, James, my blonde Cocker Spaniel, ran to greet us with his usual exuberance. As he jumped up, I saw urine go shooting across Ed's pants legs and, yes, back again (go, James!). 'Oh, I'm sooo sorry!' I said, looking at Ed's legs as he was leaving.

'Oh. That's just a little rain,' said Ed.

Yeah, right. Rain always takes a little detour through my dog's penis. And that's how I learned to appreciate the little excitement piddlers in this world. Sometimes excitement piddling can be a good thing! " —Susan

Perhaps anxious urination isn't so exciting to you. It's a nuisance, and you're sick of cleaning the carpet or floor. You simply don't share Susan's point of view (but, then, you didn't share Susan's lousy blind date, either).

WHAT TO DO FOR ANXIOUS URINATION: Ignore your dog for a full five to ten minutes after you walk in the door. Give her a chance to calm down while you go about unpacking the groceries, reading your mail, or whatever chore is first on your agenda. Enlist friends and neighbors to help you. Have them ring the doorbell or knock on the door, come in, and ignore the dog for five or ten minutes. After she calms down, greet her calmly, give her a small treat, and praise her for being a good dog. Take her out for a walk so that she can eliminate properly, and then praise her lavishly. If you get overly excited at the door when you come home, she will, too, and then you'll be back where you started.

If your dog urinates on the carpet, purchase a cleaner that removes the enzymes. Even if you think the odor is gone from your rug or floor, it isn't gone as far as your dog is concerned. Her sense of smell is far more developed than yours.

WHAT NOT TO DO FOR ANXIOUS URINATION:

Do not happily and excitedly greet your dog the minute you walk through the door and don't let visitors do it, either. Getting her excited is just going to make your problem worse. Yes, I know you're happy to see her. Your friends are probably happy to see her, too. But that doesn't mean you have to make a bad situation worse.

Never yell at your dog because, for some dogs, excitement urination is a form of submission, and you don't want to make it worse. The anxious urination will go on forever if the problem isn't addressed and remedied in a positive and calm manner.

The Dog Who Anoints Your Friends

When I was a child, my mother was mortified when a lovely British lady stopped to talk with her as she was walking past our house. The family had recently moved to the States, and her daughter was in my classroom. While they were talking, our Shepherd, who was fairly protective of my mother, lifted his leg and peed on the woman. I don't think either she or my mother ever quite recovered. Neither knew what to say after my mother apologized profusely and offered to buy the woman new stockings and shoes. The woman hurried off, and I'm not sure if they ever saw each other again. Did the dog think he was protecting my mother in some way? Maybe. Did he want to "mark" the woman as "his" because he liked her? Maybe. But it wasn't the sort of social commentary most humans would use. He wasn't deliberately being bad. He was being a dog.

Although most female dogs squat to pee, any vertical object can be the target for a male dog. If that vertical object is a human leg, and the person is being "marked" for whatever purpose the dog has in mind, it can be

socially unacceptable—not to mention embarrassing—for
the humans, that is.

 WHAT TO DO IF YOUR DOG ANOINTS SOMEONE:
If this happens, you'll need to distract the dog and
apologize. Distraction is a wonderful training tool.
The objective of distracting your dog is to give her something
else to do, since she cannot do two things at the same time
and you want to train her to do the acceptable behavior, not the
unacceptable one. If you make a fuss about how naughty she
was, she won't understand and will become frightened and confused. You can use a variety of alternate behaviors; just choose
one that works well for your dog and works well at that moment,
keeping your dog's safety in mind. For example, you can tell her
to Sit, but don't throw something for her to chase if you're near
a busy road. And, of course, offer to replace or clean the
anointed clothing.

The Gassy Dog

Okay, no one wants to talk about it, but let's face it,
everyone passes gas or breaks wind—you know, farts.

There, I've said it! It's not unusual to blame the dog. Me? No! I didn't do that! The dog did it! Sometimes, though, it really is the dog who did it, and that can lead to some really embarrassing moments. Someone once told me that her neighbor's dog used to wait until they had company, and then he'd march to the center of the living room and fart. Loudly. Sometimes, it gets even worse than that and far more embarrassing. So when you're a dog owner, equip yourself with a sense of humor and a ready wit for times like these.

When Dinner Is a Gas

"We had invited our new neighbor over to watch a movie. It was just my husband, our neighbor, and me, as well as our Doberman, Sigmund. At one point, I noticed our guest had tears in her eyes, which I thought was odd due to the fact we were watching a comedy. Later, she was fanning herself, and I asked whether she was hot. She finally said, rather embarrassed, 'I think your dog has some gas.' Lo and behold, I walked over to her side of the room and almost passed out. As dog people, we kind of laughed and apologized for not warning her ahead of time. That was the last time that particular neighbor came to visit. Now we try to limit our social set to dog people. There is less explaining and embarrassment that way. **"**

—Susan

 Yes, it can bring tears to your eyes. Not just the smell, but the embarrassment.

The Scary, Smelly Monster

"One of our dogs is a Yellow (or Southern) Black Mouthed Cur. The breed comes from Mississippi and is fiercely loyal, very athletic, and not very bright. We call ours Bubba. 'Nuf said. One day, our shining star of canine intelligence was asleep on the couch next to our Golden when he broke wind, loud enough to wake himself up. His head popped up, and as it did, he broke wind again. He got this confused look on his face, glared at me, and jumped off the couch, where again he passed gas. Tucking his tail between his legs, he headed off down the hallway, breaking wind with nearly every step. Each time he passed gas, he'd look behind him, trying desperately to see the scary monster chasing him. By the time he got to the bedroom, his ears were pinned back, his eyes were wide, and he looked for all the world as though he was being chased by the scariest monster in the universe. He jumped on the bed, dove under the covers, and waited there until my wife and I went in to convince him it was okay to come out—after we finished airing out the room and laughing. Meanwhile, our Golden simply lay on the couch and sighed. " —Paul

WHAT TO DO FOR THE GASSY DOG: First, lighten up. Dog owners will understand, and non-doggy people will understand when you explain that dogs, like people, can have gas for a variety of reasons. Next, watch your dog closely when she eats. Is she eating so fast that she's gulping air? Does she inhale one meal a day as if food were going out of style? She could easily be gulping air while she eats. Some people have used raised bowls, especially in hopes of stopping *gastric torsion* (the stomach turns around, which can be deadly), but they've discovered that it doesn't work. The best way to handle gulping, in my opinion, is to divide the day's ration into several small meals, and don't let your dog do any sort of active exercise after eating (this rule is to help prevent gastric torsion).

For gas alone, divide her food into at least two meals per day, giving her half at breakfast time and half at dinnertime. Or check whether there is an ingredient in her food that disagrees with her and gives her gas. Try to slowly change her over to another complete and balanced diet. Discuss this with your veterinarian, being sure to ask what you don't want to see in the ingredients list on the label. Or, perhaps, she has eaten something she shouldn't have eaten while you weren't looking.

WHAT NOT TO DO FOR THE GASSY DOG: Don't ignore recurring gas because it may be a digestive problem. And for heaven's sake, do not turn to your guests and say, "Pull my finger."

PART 3

SOCIAL SNAFUS

DOGS ARE DOGS, AND THE SOONER

you learn to appreciate this, the better. Their behaviors are perfectly normal—for dogs. When they live among us, we have to teach them what is appropriate behavior around people. Most humans don't want their butts sniffed, some don't want their faces licked, and most would prefer it if a dog were not wrapped firmly around their legs in a romantic embrace. If you and your dog want to enjoy life together with a full circle of friends, read on.

MOST ANNOYING BEHAVIOR: **Humping**

On a hot first date or that big dinner at your boss's house, nothing gets the evening started quite like a dog humping you at the door. You may have wanted to expand your social horizon, but chances are, this wasn't what you had in mind. We've all seen dogs display humping behavior, often to our embarrassment.

WHAT HUMPING MEANS: Dogs hump for a variety of reasons. Sometimes, they are in it for the fun, the entertainment value, and the reaction they get from the guests. Yep, humping is the floor show, and they're not stupid. Not only do they enjoy doing it, there's the added reward of the human reaction. What could be better from the dog's point of view? Sex hormones also influence this behavior as well. Intact dogs who have experienced sex are likely to hump, even after having been neutered. The testosterone kicks in, and that's when the hormones influence the behavior. It's also not unusual for a dog to hump a more submissive dog in the household. You may well see puppies humping littermates; this is play behavior. Really. Another less frequent cause of humping can be irritation or itching in the genital area, so it's possible that, after you've thought about the other possible motives, a trip to the veterinarian is in order.

It's a Ball

"A young lady was interested in adopting a rescue dog and wanted to check out the breed. She fell in love with Arthur, my imported Old English Sheepdog from the United Kingdom. Well, Arthur loved two things in this world: Any pink pig toy, no matter how large or small. No pink pig was ever safe. As big as he was, he would gently weasel his way up to wherever the toy was and very gently take it—even if it was in a baby's grasp. But the other thing was a ball. If it was a ball, it was his.

That summer, the young lady accompanied me on the New England dog show circuit. We stayed in the hotel room, and she brought Arthur a red rubber ball. He was ecstatic! Imagine this ninety-pound full-coated Old English Sheepdog in the hotel room throwing this ball into the air and pouncing on it, bouncing it off the walls and catching it, and so on. He loved this red rubber ball she had given him. And then it rolled under the bed. The young lady made the mistake, given that Arthur was a fully intact two-and-a-half-year-old young male. She bent over on hands and knees to get that ball out from under the bed and Arthur was . . . oh, boy! She was so shocked at his grasping her from behind and my grasping at him that we both fell over laughing! At that point, Arthur had turned his mind back to the red rubber ball that had rolled out from under the bed and was back to "Ball? Oh, boy! A ball!!" and never skipped a beat, bouncing it off the walls again. " —Lea

 WHAT TO DO FOR HUMPING: To stop humping behavior, use a verbal interrupter. You can simply say, "'Uh!" as an interrupter sound, or call the dog to you and give the offending canine an alternate behavior to perform, such as his default behavior, which may be Sit or

Down. You can also teach him a trick—anything that will distract him from his favorite hobby.

Dirty Dancing

Judith Swan, who dances with her rescue Schipperkes, has incorporated humping behavior into one of her routines. Judith and one of the dogs dance to "Hitching a Ride." The dog hangs on to her leg but doesn't hump. So, Judith has taught the little Schipperke a variation of the behavior by putting it on cue and altering it just a bit. That was a very creative solution to what might have been an embarrassing situation. Now the dog only does it upon request and isn't humping but holding on and getting rewarded for it. It's a satisfactory outcome for dog and owner. And it's a very entertaining one as well. Learn more about Canine Musical Freestyle at www.worldcaninefreestyle.org.

WHAT NOT TO DO ABOUT HUMPING: Don't laugh. (And don't offer your guest a cigarette after the "performance.") Laughing will only reinforce unwanted behavior, and some dogs really love an audience. Remember that many of these behaviors appear only when there's company in the house because it's pretty much guaranteed to get the owner's attention. Don't be afraid to tell your guests that you're trying to change unwanted behavior and ask them, before they come to your house, to please ignore the behavior because you want to extinguish it and replace it with something acceptable. Enlisting their help will aide in the retraining of your canine exhibitionist—and may even forewarn your guests. Also, be aware that there may be an *extinction burst,* or an increase in the unwanted behavior. But if this happens, don't vary from your chosen course of action to change the behavior, as tempting as that may be. Once the extinction burst is over, that should be the end of it. Don't punish your dog for humping, either. That can create worse problems than humping.

The Conga Line

❝ I have a menagerie of dogs. Three Beagles, three Schipperkes, and one Greyhound. Over the years, I've had many different dogs, but this current pack o' hounds is the most humorous. Or maybe I'm just slowing down and taking time to enjoy their personalities. For example, it never fails that when I have company, and usually non-doggie company, the pups take the time to assemble the canine conga line.

It starts with Alfred, my two-year-old Schipperke, in the front of the line. Usually following is George, my nine-year-old tan-and-white Beagle, who decides to hump Alfred. The line is usually made a bit longer by Lola, the twelve-year-old Beagle, doing her best to hang on and hump! Sometimes, Lucy, my two-year-old rescue Schipperke, decides she wants to get into the act too, bringing the total up to four dogs doing the hump dance. Many times, I've tried to get a picture, but usually when I get up, the line disassembles, the players all expecting a lovely treat of some sort for their talent and hard work! Thankfully, my pastor and his wife revealed a huge sense of humor when they witnessed this floor show.

The one time I tried to break it up, I moved the second dog (the humper, George), and by the time I pushed the third one away, George had "latched on" to Alfred again! I did get them to stop though. I've found that when the dogs start playing, I need to keep an eye on George. When he starts to make his move, I just correct him before anything ever starts, by using a verbal No! That way, there are seldom any problems. It seems that George, being the dominant Beagle in the pack, is the one that everyone takes their cues from. If George does it, the others will follow. If I can stop the lead dog, I can stop the behavior."

—Patty

No matter how you look at it, humping is a perfectly normal behavior for a dog. Although you can use distraction techniques or your default behavior, sooner or later, that urge will be there for reasons sometimes known only to the dog. In these cases, it's best to retain your sense of humor.

 MOST ANNOYING BEHAVIOR: **Help for the Barking Dog**

My neighbor works all day, and I can hear her dog barking constantly. I have a home office, and it's hard for me to concentrate when all I hear is this endless noise. I also feel sorry for the dog. You could call him the worst dog in the neighborhood, but I just think he's the saddest one. I don't know what to do. And I could use a cure for this constant headache I have now, too!

Talking with your neighbor is a good idea. She's probably not aware that her dog is barking all day because he's happy to see her and stops barking when he hears her car pull into the driveway or her walking to the door. It's likely he thinks his barking is calling her home, and when she arrives, he knows that it did. Your neighbor needs to either come home at lunchtime to walk and play with the dog or hire someone to do it. Or, if you're so inclined, you could volunteer. That would help to ease the dog's loneliness and boredom.

WHAT BARKING MEANS: A dog who barks constantly is trying to tell you something. A little barking goes a long way. A lot of barking is just irritating. Sometimes, barking connotes stress; other times, it means there's someone at the door or on your property; and still other times, it's sheer joy, or another dog is barking and your dog feels compelled to join the conversation. It could also mean that your dog is alone and frightened and wants someone to give him some attention.

WHAT TO DO IF YOUR DOG BARKS: Before you leave the house, you can put him in a room with a comfy crate, complete with soft bed and a cuddly toy (with the door to the crate open, please) so that he can snuggle down for naps. He should also have a hollow toy stuffed with either a biscuit, peanut butter, or some flavored doggy toothpaste to keep him occupied. You can also leave a radio or TV on so that he hears the sound of human voices. Dogs need companionship, and he must be awfully bored and lonely all by himself, all day long. Always make sure fresh water is available, that he isn't hungry, and that he has a place to eliminate if he can't "hold it" until you get home.

You can also train your dog to bark on cue, which can help resolve the problem, because it puts you in control of the barking. This way he can still bark, but only when you say it's okay. If you need more help, seek out a board-certified veterinary behaviorist, a Ph.D. behaviorist, or a certified animal behavior consultant to help you resolve the issue.

WHAT NOT TO DO IF YOUR DOG BARKS: Don't yell at a barking dog. You may think you're telling him to be quiet, but he thinks you're joining him in a bark-fest. Although some people may recommend debarking the dog (surgery to cut his vocal cords), training is what he needs, not unnecessary surgery. And remember: dogs who have been debarked can still bark; they just sound hoarse. Some owners who live in apartment complexes debark their dogs because they believe it's the last resort before the landlord or the condo association tells them to get rid of the barking dog or face fines or eviction. A very few frustrated owners will try to give their barking dog to an animal shelter as a last resort. These are not the solutions. Training your dog is.

Most Annoying Behavior: **The Aggressive Dog**

Some dogs can be aggressive toward people; some can be aggressive toward other dogs. Or you could have hit the jackpot with your dog, and he can exhibit both behaviors. There are several causes of aggressive (also called *reactive*) behavior. Sometimes it's fear, sometimes it's territorial, and sometimes it's *redirected aggression,* which means that if a dog can't get near the person or thing he wants to attack, he will attack whoever or whatever is close to him. Dogs who are aggressive toward people may think they're protecting their property, including their owners. Other causes of aggression may be a dog who is stressed or bred improperly. Signs of aggression include barking, snarling, snapping, and baring his teeth, which usually goes along with a snarl or growl. The worst form of aggression is biting.

Dog Park Blues

❝There's a state park near my house. They have a dog-friendly area of the park, although, of course, the rule is that dogs have to be on a leash. (We'll let that go for a moment, because most of the dogs, including my own, tend not to be. How can you do agility and obedience recalls on a leash?) About a football field's distance away is a reflecting pond. Oh and of course I have to mention that my Yorkshire Terrier, Bun, has a 99 percent solid recall, and at the time of this incident, he was competing at the Open level of AKC Agility. We had been working for about fifteen minutes on a small sequence of jumps, and everything was going well. So my radar (my Bun-dar) was not on as it should have been. Well, you also need to know that Bun has had a vendetta against big dogs since the day I brought him home. It's part of his whole Napoleon complex. Suddenly, seemingly for no reason, Bun took off. Naturally, I called after him, and he didn't come. So, in my panic, I did the last thing you should do—I started running after him. Needless to say, he's a lot faster than I am, especially when he's on a mission. So I charged across the park in the direction of the reflecting pond. That's when I caught a glimpse of the source of all the excitement. A placid old Lab was taking a dip in the pond. I say a 'glimpse' because the next minute, I stubbed my foot, tripped, and fell, pell-mell and headfirst, into the reflecting pond (grace is not a family attribute)! The pond, by the way, is frequented by swans and wild geese and isn't very well drained. After a moment, I gathered my wits and stood up. The goose dung was hanging off of me, and I must have looked like the creature from the black lagoon. From this vantage point, I saw my crazy Yorkshire Terrier hanging from the mouth of this Lab. Naturally, Bun was spitting and thrashing about. The poor Lab, on the other hand, was standing there, very still and placid, wagging his tail and acting like this was a very agreeable game of fetch. The Lab's owner was doubled over in hysterical laughter. Even though the Lab had decided Bun was a good retrieving bumper, there was not a scratch on my Terrier. Fortunately for both of us, the Lab and his owner had a good sense of humor! " —Rena

Actually, I can only laugh because, thankfully, little Mr. Bun wasn't killed. His attitude could have turned him into a snack for a large dog. Big dog/little dog aggression is a serious problem, and Bun was certainly being aggressive. It doesn't have to be the big dog's fault. You're responsible for your dog's behavior no matter what his size. This is also a good example of how even the most well-trained dog will take off and not respond to a recall if something else seems more important to him. In this case, it was the Labrador Retriever enjoying his outing. It is fortunate, too, that Retrievers have a soft mouth so that they don't injure the birds they retrieve, hence the rowdy little Terrier came away unscathed.

WHAT TO DO IF YOUR DOG IS AGGRESSIVE:

It would take an entire book to tell you about aggression in great detail and how to manage it in its many forms. You can find some great books in the Resources section at the back of this book. For now, here are some helpful tips.

The first thing you should do is to take him to a veterinarian to be sure that there isn't some underlying medical or other reason for his behavior. Ask your veterinarian to do a complete workup, including a thyroid panel. If your dog is sick, he can display symptoms that could easily be mistaken for aggression. If, however, all tests rule out a medical cause, you are dealing with aggression and will need professional help from a board-certified veterinary behaviorist, a Ph.D. behaviorist (someone who has earned a doctorate in animal behavior), or a certified dog behavior consultant. (Check out www.iaabc.org for one in your area.) You can also find a list of trainers at www.clickertraining.com.

Spaying or neutering your dog will help most aggression problems. Whatever you do, don't yell at your dog or punish him, because it will only make matters worse. Behaviorists have discovered that aggression begets aggression. Use gentle positive training methods like clicker training.

You'll need to make sure that all people and other animals are safe if your dog is truly aggressive. Management is key. If your dog can't be trusted around strangers, be sure that he's in a separate room with toys and a radio as well as a bowl of fresh water while you have guests in your home. He'll be happy, and everyone will be safe.

If you take your dog out for a walk, a leash isn't enough. Dogs on a leash can believe that they gain status from being attached to the owner via the leash. You have to be vigilant and watch his body language to be sure that he isn't allowed to become aggressive toward people or other dogs. If he gets aggressive, use distraction techniques. Give him an alternate behavior to perform. If you see someone coming toward you with a dog, cross the street or turn and walk in another direction to avoid an encounter. And remember that you are responsible for whatever your dog does, and that includes the legal ramifications of a dog bite.

Be patient. And know that you will always be managing your dog throughout his life, taking care that he doesn't become aggressive toward another dog or person, even after he has been retrained. It will require a lifetime of careful management.

 ## WHAT NOT TO DO FOR AGGRESSION:

Don't take your aggressive dog to dog parks where he will become the neighborhood bully, terrorizing the other dogs. When he's around other dogs, carefully supervise him. It would be best to seek out the help of a behaviorist if possible. Be careful of any training class you choose, especially if you have an aggressive dog. Be sure the trainer is one who really understands the importance of not increasing the fear and aggression in an aggressive dog.

Popular Doesn't Always
Mean Better

"I took my aggressive dog to a seminar conducted by a well-known dog trainer. During the seminar, she asked about issues. I'd made it clear beforehand that we were attending only to get Bongo out for socialization. She asked us to come up so she could talk about aggression. I spoke of his main issues, particularly not liking his feet touched. She pointed out the stress signals he was showing. Then, out of the blue, she reached around him and grabbed his foot! Of course he gave an inhibited bite, and she immediately hit him with an empty soda bottle, saying that's how she punishes dogs. At that moment, he proceeded to sit on her lap and expressed his anal glands. Obviously, he was terrified, and she was certainly being both aggressive and unfair. And note that the bite he gave was inhibited. He was warning her and protecting himself.

I recognize now that she was setting him up from the start. Lesson learned. I spent the next few minutes calming him and listening to her talk about how dangerous he was. Everyone took a break, and we went outside to regroup. We surprised everyone when we came back and finished the class, practicing Come and Stay our way and ending on a positive note. We left with our heads held up high; we had been tricked, but we still completed all the exercises beautifully. "

—Anna

This also illustrates that just because a trainer is well known doesn't mean he or she is a good trainer or right for your dog. It just means that person may be very good at public relations.

When Your Dog Snarls or Bites

If your dog snarls, consider that a warning either toward you or someone else. If he has true *bite inhibition* (biting, but not breaking the skin), and you recognize aggressive body language (his hackles are up, his posture changes, ears are forward or back, and you see his eyes narrow), he may snarl in a menacing tone or snap, which is the warning that a real bite may be forthcoming.

 WHAT TO DO IF YOUR DOG SNARLS: To avoid a snarl leading to a bite, give your dog calming signals. Do what he would do to another dog; that is, yawn, turn your head, blink your eyes. Do not stare straight into your dog's eyes. He will consider that a challenge, and you don't want to put him in that position and escalate his stress and/or fear, which is causing the snarling. Again, try distraction as a way of diffusing his stress. If another person is nearby, warn him that your dog is aggressive. If he has a dog with him, ask him to please get his dog out of range of your dog while you try to regain your dog's attention.

If pushed too far, or if physically hurt by someone or something, your dog may bite. If he doesn't break the skin, he's
exhibiting wonderful bite inhibition. Consider this a serious
warning.

 WHAT TO DO IF YOUR DOG BITES: If your dog
bites and breaks the skin, the person who was bitten
will have to have a tetanus shot if the doctor feels
it's necessary. Most people aren't up to date on their tetanus
shots. If your dog bites someone, you are responsible. Part of
your responsibility is paying for that person's medical bills,
offering help, and certainly apologizing. Immediately remove
your dog and offer to get medical help for the person. Because
most people carry a cell phone today, that should be fairly easy
to accomplish. Here is one very important thing you need to
remember, along with the fact that you should be working with
positive training and a behavior consultant before your dog's
problem reaches this point: If your dog hasn't had an up-to-date
rabies vaccination, he will be quarantined by your state and
may have to be put to sleep. That's why rabies shots are man-
dated by state law throughout the United States and why it is so

important to treat an aggression situation before it escalates. Get your dog his rabies shots, and get behavioral help for your biting dog.

Is It Okay to Let My Dog Give Me Love Bites?

 My dog sometimes gives me love bites. Is that okay?

 Ahhh, love bites. I think what we really want to discuss is something called bite inhibition. There are two kinds of bites: the kind that breaks the skin, and the kind that doesn't, when the dog is politely warning you that you'd better knock it off now before he really gets angry and a human ends up in the emergency room.

Some dogs are what is generally called *mouthy*. Retrievers are known for this. They always have to have something in their mouths: a toy, a stuffed animal, or something else to substitute for that game bird they were bred to carry but not injure. This is known as having a *soft mouth*, when they gently carry something. With other dogs, if you say, "Show Me," they will lead you by the hand, taking your hand in their mouths ever so gently. I had one of those. I found it charming. But we're not going to be talking about that. Okay, well, we just did. A little.

The Peacemaker

"I had taken my cat (a fourteen-pound monster named Rodney) to the vet for his shots and a checkup. Picture it: He's sitting calmly in his carrier and across the lobby from us is a huge Saint Bernard, just lying lazily on the floor. From the examination room behind us, a German Shepherd emerges. Suddenly, the Saint Bernard is on his feet, and the two dogs are growling at each other with their hackles raised, and their owners are trying to hold on to their leashes. My cat, who had been calmly grooming his paw this entire time, looks up at the melee and simply meows (he doesn't hiss or spit, just meows). The two large dogs, who could easily make an hors d'oeuvre out of my cat, both dropped to the floor in fright as Rodney resumed grooming himself. If the vet and the two dog owners hadn't been witnesses, no one would believe me! " —Linda

 Who knows what the cat said to the dogs. They're not talking. But it was certainly effective.

TOP 10

MOST ANNOYING BEHAVIOR: **The Possessive Dog**

You know who I'm talking about: The *possessive* or *resource-guarding* dog is the one who won't let you pick up his favorite toy or go near his favorite chair, and so on. Resource guarding often can manifest itself in guarding the owner (the source of all good things) so that no one else can come near his chosen human (or, as he probably prefers to think of his owner, my personal slave). This is love taken too far.

Relationships can be tricky. If the owner and dog are closely bonded, the dog can see a new friend or spouse as an interloper on his territory, and that includes not just his home but also his owner. The owner provides all good things: food, water, love, play, walks, and so on. The dog does not want to lose those resources. The problem may be compounded when the owner continues patterns, such as feeding the dog first, because this is just part of the owner's normal routine. The owner fails to consult the other person who has entered his or her life to see whether this is okay or whether they should change the established routine.

A Napoleon Complex?

There is a famous story about Josephine Bonaparte, who had a Pug named Fortune. When Josephine married Napoleon, it's said that on their wedding night, Fortune refused to allow Napoleon to sleep with them in the bed. To make his point, Fortune bit Napoleon. Napoleon was forced to share their bed with Fortune when Josephine stated, "If the

Pug doesn't sleep in our bed, neither do I!" It's said that later, Josephine used Fortune to send Napoleon secret messages. To the educated dog owner, Fortune was resource guarding, and Josephine was his resource. It's nice to know that they were able to overcome the problem.

 WHAT TO DO FOR RESOURCE GUARDING: If your dog is guarding you as the resource, calm the dog down and don't yell. Aggression begets aggression, and there's no sense in making a bad situation worse. With all dogs who are resource guarders, you have to move slowly and calmly.

If you have a new spouse or roommate, have that person feed the dog so he knows that good things come from the other person as well as from you.

In situations when the dog is on the floor and guarding you, turn and walk out of the room for a minute, thereby removing the object of his obsession. If there is one particular area of the house where the dog seems to become the most obsessive in his resource guarding, buy a pheromone diffuser and plug it in.

The release of pheromones into the air will help calm the dog. (Pheromone diffusers are also helpful to use in an area of the house where two dogs aren't getting along.)

If your dog has taken to guarding things, remember that your dog's favorite sofa isn't "his"; it's yours. If there's something specific that he guards, remove the object if possible so that he isn't put into a situation where he thinks he needs to "guard" it. This doesn't mean his toys. He's entitled to have his toys, and this is where "Trade You" comes in handy. Teach him to share his toys or to give you his toy when you say, "Trade you."

You can prevent resource guarding by starting while your dog is a puppy. Along with the usual training for Sit, Stay, and Down, train your puppy (or adult dog) to Trade You for something he would consider more valuable than the object he prizes (see Part 1). If it's his food bowl that he guards, for example, drop pieces of kibble into the bowl while he's eating so that he learns that there's always more and you have it for him.

WHAT NOT TO DO FOR RESOURCE GUARDING:

Don't yell at the dog or reach for him. Consider a growl a warning. Watch his body posture. If hackles are raised, do not try to approach him. Keep your own body posture as relaxed as possible, staying a safe distance away. Using some of noted dog trainer Turid Rugaas's Calming Signals can help: yawn, turn your head to the side, and avoid staring at the dog. Remember that aggression will only beget aggression. And don't think that if your dog is small he won't bite. He has teeth and is perfectly capable of biting. Get thee to a behaviorist or behavior consultant.

MOST ANNOYING BEHAVIOR: **The Crotch-Sniffer**

What do you do if your dog seems entirely interested in sniffing people's . . . um . . . privates? Or when you're on a much-anticipated first date and your Dream Man's Doberman sticks his nose where it doesn't belong: in your crotch? As far as the dog's concerned, this is perfectly normal greeting behavior. However, you are not a dog, and this is not the way you really expect to be greeted by someone new, even if he does have four legs and a tail!

WHAT TO DO FOR CROTCH-SNIFFING: For every unwanted behavior, a dog should be given an alternate behavior to perform. If your dog is known to crotch-sniff, prepare your guests ahead of time. When someone arrives and your dog is ready to assume the position, so to speak, ask your dog to perform a behavior like shaking hands or bringing you a favorite toy. Even asking him to Sit or Lie Down will help.

WHAT NOT TO DO FOR CROTCH-SNIFFING: Do not scream; you'll only frighten the dog. After all, he's only exhibiting normal dog behavior. It's just not normal human behavior. If you are the one being sniffed, don't jump backward or run because the dog will think the game is on. And, even though the situation can be embarrassing for humans, try not to laugh because it will only reinforce the behavior.

PART 4

BAD TABLE MANNERS

EVERYONE HAS TO EAT TO SURVIVE,

but sometimes food issues can cause various problems for us and our dogs, whether it's the kind of food we feed, a dog's food fussiness, or a dog who steals food from the table. While feeding your dog sounds pretty straightforward—just open bag and pour—when it comes to your dog, too many choices of food and feeding methods can be confusing, leading you into temptation and your dog into trouble.

Feeding Patterns and Behavior

When you bring a new puppy home, she will probably be eating four meals a day. At six months of age, you can reduce the frequency to three meals a day. At a year, I believe there are several advantages to feeding your adult dog twice a day instead of once a day, as most owners do.

I prefer to divide a dog's meals into half in the morning and half at dinnertime, because the food can be utilized better over twenty-four hours and digested more consistently over that time. If your dog stops eating, you'll know sooner because twenty-four hours will not have to pass before you feed him again. This allows you to more quickly note an oncoming illness and take him to the veterinarian for a more rapid diagnosis. Plus, from a behavior standpoint, the dog will likely be eating breakfast and dinner when you eat and is therefore less likely to beg during your meals.

The "Perfect" Dog Food

I have been contacted many times by owners of perfectly healthy dogs doing well on whatever food they had been eating. The insecure owner will be convinced that he or she has made the wrong choice and will switch to someone else's favorite way of feeding. Unfortunately, if the new food isn't right for the dog, she can become quite ill.

First of all, there is no such thing as the "perfect" food. Every dog is different depending upon activity level, size, digestive system, and taste buds, too! What dogs need is a diet that's complete and balanced for their species. So just because a stranger who e-mails or has a website says that a type of food is perfect, it doesn't mean it's true. Or if someone tells you that you should feed only cooked food or raw food and if you don't, you don't love your dog, well, that's just absurd. What someone else chooses to do may be something else entirely. And that is their choice.

There are three opinions of what is right: *commercial food* (kibble in a bag or food in a can or tin); *cooked food* (a home-prepared cooked diet, which must be carefully balanced); or a *raw diet* (a home-prepared diet with raw meat as a major component). Although there are people who swear by a raw diet, it must be carefully balanced for your dog. Preparing raw meat can be deadly for someone who is immune compromised. Plus, if the dog eating raw meat kisses you or anyone else, especially on the lips, salmonella can be spread to the human. The topic can become so volatile that some Internet lists have banned the topic, while others have been created just to talk about one of those forms of feeding. I recommend feeding your dog a complete and balanced commercial diet from a reputable company.

The Benefits of Commercial Food

Feeding your dog a commercial diet isn't just about time and cost. Pet food companies hire the very best veterinary nutritionists to research and create a complete and balanced diet for dogs. It's best to ask your veterinarian for a recommendation since poor-quality food can be lacking in nutrients or it might be made with inferior-quality ingredients. The wrong diet can lead to behavior problems such as acting out, being hyperactive, and having trouble focusing. It can also lead to a dull coat and bad breath that practically knocks you over. You might need to do a little research to find the right food for your dog, but once you find the right one, there's no reason to change. And remember, fresh water should be available twenty-four hours a day.

MOST ANNOYING BEHAVIOR: **Help for the Begging Dog**

 Whenever I have a dinner party, my dog's tail is in my guests' plates. He sits under the table, begs and whines, and is just a general nuisance. What can I do?

Never feed your dog from the table because you will not only be creating bad habits but you will be unbalancing his diet. Make sure other people in your household know never to feed him from the table or they will be undoing all of your hard work.

Your dog needs to be taught to behave properly when you are at the table and that extends to when you have guests over. There shouldn't be any begging at the table, so be sure to tell your guests not to encourage it. (Consistency is important, and some people think it's okay to feed the dog from the table.) If it's not okay at your house (it will only unbalance his diet and help him gain unwanted weight), then by all means say so to your guests! Your dog can, after eating his own meal, lie on his rug or dog bed and play with a toy until everyone is finished with their meal. To correct begging behavior, buy your dog a mat of his own and tell him to go to his place and Lie Down. Teach him by repetitious experience that, after dinner, he can have his treat.

When Your Dog Steals Food

Some self-service pups have a hard time resisting the wonderful smells emanating from the oven, the stove, or the grocery bag and will gleefully go *counter shopping*. Be sure to help your dog behave properly by putting those groceries away as soon as you bring them into the house. Don't encourage temptation.

Dumb as a Fox

"Our very first homebred Newfoundland, Andrew—better known as RooRoo—was rather interesting. We'd automatically start talking baby talk when discussing him, because 'RooRoo wasn't bery big on bwains, but he was berry wubbable.' When we thought about things he did, we realized he was dumb like a fox!

We lived in a bilevel-style house. We'd be eating dinner, and Roo would run to the steps, barking as if someone were at the door. We'd get up to check and, followed by the other Newfs, go to the door. Meanwhile, RooRoo would go around the other way and the table would be cleaned off by the time we got back. I'm rather ashamed to admit how many times he got away with that one! "

—Lynne

Left to their own devices, we know that dogs will steal food from the kitchen counter or the table, and will eat just about anything that isn't nailed down and won't eat them first. In that respect they're like little kids.

Food, Glorious Food!

"I have a picture of my poor refrigerator after it was raided by two Portuguese Water Dogs. How the dogs survived this refrigerator incident, I have no idea—they ate a pound of bacon, a slice of ham steak, a piece of leftover fish, a carton of cream cheese, an unopened block of American cheese, a package of ready-made coleslaw, one zucchini, some tomatoes, one English muffin, and undoubtedly other things I did not remember were in there! And they didn't even bloat.

There have been other incidents as well, but none quite this serious, as I don't keep much in the refrigerator anymore. The effort to find a lockout method was another matter. One lock worked for a while, but they finally figured it out last week while I was away. Would you like two charming Portuguese Water Dogs as a gift?" —Ruth

💬 Uh, no, I wouldn't. Owning a Portuguese Water Dog requires more than just a sense of humor. It's sort of like owning a Lamborghini—it's going to require a lot of maintenance just to stay ahead of those four-legged little geniuses. It was bad enough when my tiny Yorkshire Terrier backed himself up to the refrigerator, stuck his butt under the door, and tried to get it open. Fortunately, weighing only five pounds, he didn't have enough muscle to accomplish his goal. Plenty of canine Houdinis have even opened locks on gates or crates and let other dogs out, and I remember one little dog who could open an antique chest with a trick lock. Never underestimate the intelligence of a dog. Although not all them are that clever, yours may surprise you someday, so don't say I didn't warn you!

Although not all dogs will figure out how to open the refrigerator, plenty of dogs like to counter-surf.

WHAT TO DO FOR COUNTER-SURFERS: Put all groceries away the minute you get home from the supermarket. And never leave anything out on the counter unattended. Even if you stay close, don't leave anything close to the edge of the counter, even for a second. If you're making a sandwich, your little darling can reach up to the counter, sneak the meat out of your sandwich, and be back on her bed before you return from putting the mustard away.

WHAT NOT TO DO FOR COUNTER-SURFERS: If you have a confirmed counter-surfer, be sure she doesn't have access to the kitchen when you're not at home. You might want to keep her in a safe room with a radio on, some comfy bedding, and some interesting and challenging toys to play with. This way she won't find ways to amuse herself in the kitchen that you won't find funny. Even when you are at home, if you know that your furry friend is a counter-surfer, don't turn your back on the dog if food is on the counter, even if it's just for a moment. It's simplest if you train the dog to Stay or keep her otherwise engaged.

Happy Holidays

"We had a lovely Christmas day in sunny California. It started at 5:00 AM with the ritual defrosting of the turkey in the kitchen sink. (Someone had too much red wine the night before and forgot to do it then.) Meanwhile, due to the turkey's reluctance to thaw, dinner was late—very late—but eventually, the turkey was ready. The poor dogs had literally been tortured all afternoon by the wonderful smells as it roasted away in the oven. Finally, I pulled the turkey out and placed it on the counter to rest and prepared the rest of the meal. Our dogs never touch food on the counter or beg at the table because they are pretty sure that they are going get some anyway. Having this knowledge has made me very relaxed during food preparation.

Our dogs know all about Christmas day, but for the last two years we were invited to other places to eat, and the poor dogs have been shortchanged.

This year, what with the toys, the chewies, and all the fun of wrapping paper, they were wound pretty tight.

As luck would have it, and probably due to my aching head, a few items were a tad late making it to the table. My husband, John, and I were sitting in the family room resting up for the eventual feast and waiting for the last items to cook, when Toby ran to my husband and barked once, loudly, right in his face. Then Toby wheeled and raced back to the kitchen. John looked at me and said, 'Gee, that was odd; maybe we should investigate.' As we peeked into the kitchen, there was a horrible sight. Short, chubby Lily was stretched up on her tiptoes as far as she could go, her front legs braced against a kitchen drawer. With a lot of stretching, she had just been able to sink her teeth into the far end of the turkey. When she realized that we were looking at her, not even the Wrath of Mom would get her to let go of that turkey. She looked guilty, sorry, and slightly crazy all at the same time. I think the smell of the turkey roasting all day had pushed her to the edge of reason. The look she gave Toby was pure evil, and he will be paying for tattling for a very long time to come. "

—Emily

The Dog Who Eats Strange Things

From time to time all dogs will extend their culinary palette to include things like grass or mulch, but when it goes beyond that, to regularly consuming rocks, paper towels, or the bark off the trees, the condition is called *pica*. While it may be a psychological problem, your veterinarian should first rule out any organic cause such as an incomplete diet or a problem with the esophagus. Once organic causes are ruled out, consider whether it could be from a shortage of exercise, boredom, or loneliness. Sometimes, it's just a remnant of puppyhood, when the little one was exploring everything by using her mouth (which is logical when you don't have hands). A colleague told me that Newfoundlands will eat tree bark, a hard-wired behavior that goes back to when they had to do that for survival. Eating rocks, stone, socks, and similar items is very dangerous for your dog and can lead to surgery to remove the offending object.

 WHAT TO DO FOR PICA: To avoid the temptation, give your dog an assortment of toys and initiate safe games so she won't become bored and eat things she shouldn't consume. Dogs are like children, going through a stage where everything goes into their mouths. Only dogs don't have much of a choice for alternative testing methods. Keeping a watchful eye and teaching her to Drop It or Leave It will be very helpful in these situations.

The Dog Who Eats Poop

If you think you're the only owner whose dog has a penchant for eating poop, think again: there's even a word for eating excrement—*coprophagia*. Sounds sort of like an operatic aria, doesn't it? Well, the only thing operatic about it is the blood-curdling scream from the owner who sees this happening. Not all that much is known about coprophagia, although there are plenty of guesses. Is the dog getting something more from the food the second time around? Is it true recycling? Most puppies do it, but they usually grow out of it. Shih Tzu puppies are notorious for it.

 WHAT TO DO FOR COPROPHAGIA: Keep a watchful eye and clean up before the dog has a chance to eat the excrement. There are products you can sprinkle on poop to make it taste bad, but there are always going to be dogs who think of those products as condiments. Oftentimes, puppies and dogs who like to play with their own excrement come from kennel situations where they've never been given toys and have never truly learned to play. The best you can do is to be gentle with them and slowly teach them about playing and toys.

That Katrina Chowhound

"I fell in love with a middle-aged, small southern dog named Abbe. She was tan and white with an upbeat personality despite finding herself in a horrid predicament following Hurricane Katrina. The twenty-six-pound, six-year-old Sheltie/Corgi mix was fished out of murky water in Louisiana a couple of days after Katrina struck. I had gone there as a volunteer to help the animals. One day a guy called in as mad as can be and said, 'There's a dog outside of here swimming around and barking constantly. If you don't get it out of here within thirty minutes, I'm gonna shoot it.' The animal control officer caught her and brought her to the giant makeshift shelter that Noah's Wish and Slidell Animal Control established on high ground. She was one of well over one thousand inhabitants.

Abbe was one of about fifty or sixty dogs I walked daily during my rescue work. Despite the noisy, crowded, and exceptionally humid environment and being crated 24/7, she remained upbeat and never quit wagging her tail. She wore no tags, and no owner was found. I brought her home to the dismay of my wife who thought our German Shepherd was enough. Abbe, we quickly learned, not only wasn't housetrained, but she had contracted everything imaginable in Louisiana—from skin-allergy dermatitis to an ear infection and heartworm, which we treated with the financial help of Noah's Wish.

My adult daughters call her Junkyard and Corndog (the latter label because she resembles a corndog; the former, because she chews up every loose thing she finds on the floor, from towels to a gel ice wrap). Recently, she took her pillaging to an all-new low while I was in Mexico on a dog-rescue trip. Before leaving, I had left extra cash out for any potential emergency. My wife had put three hundred dollars in the pocket of her bathrobe, which she'd laid on an ottoman. Abbe spotted the bills in the bathrobe, pulled them onto the floor, and started chewing. It wasn't long before she'd destroyed the entire wad, leaving the remains in tatters on the floor. My wife frantically grabbed the tiny pieces of paper off the rug and placed them in a plastic bag. For the next several days, she recouped more from the dog's daily deposits outside, carefully cleaning each piece.

It turns out that if you send mutilated currency to the Department of Treasury, Bureau of Engraving and Printing, it will attempt to reassemble the scraps and reimburse you for everything identifiable. We sent every shred—there were dozens—via registered mail, along with a humorous letter. Within several days, we received a receipt and a case number. The notice said it would be 'some time' until our case would be addressed and rated it as a Grade 2: 'Complete, almost complete, or easily identified portions of notes, containing little amounts of foreign matter.'

Fortunately, the money finally arrived and Abbe has managed to shed the potentially fatal heart-worms after a ten-month battle that forced us to keep her inactive for two months following two rounds of treatment.

More than one person has asked me, in jest, 'Is there such a thing as a Louisiana lemon law? Maybe you can exchange her for another model.' No way. Her spirit is the psychological salve for a natural disaster that changed my emotional land-scape forever. " —Ranny

It's comforting to know that you can recoup the shredded legal tender. It's also comforting to know that I don't have to personally piece it together along with the "foreign matter." On the other hand, if your child tries to tell you that the dog ate his homework, you can always tell him that if the government can piece money together, he can produce the shredded paper and piece his homework together.

WHAT TO DO FOR A CHOWHOUND: Dog-proof your home as if you were child-proofing it. You'd be amazed at the places dogs can get into and the things they can find while they're exploring. You'd even be amazed at how many expensive shoes your dog can mistake for a chewy toy. Keep poisonous items out of reach and lock your cabinets. You really are better safe than sorry, and so is your dog.

 WHAT NOT TO DO FOR A CHOWHOUND: Don't leave valuables where the dog can reach them. And if you see your dog chewing something valuable or offensive, don't yell at the dog; tell her to Leave It. Better to plan ahead and avoid the problem before it happens by dog-proofing your house.

The Bulimic Dog

Food can cause all sorts of interesting reactions from dogs, just as it can from people. Sometimes, even more so. I often hear from owners who have had their appetites appeased after seeing a beloved dog gobble down her meal, regurgitate it, and then eat it again—gives real meaning to the term "predigested food," doesn't it? Why do dogs do this? Maybe the food didn't hit her right the first time, or maybe she wanted to have it premoistened with her own stomach juices. Occasional regurgitation is perfectly normal for many dogs, especially type-A canines who may be under more stress than other dogs.

 WHAT TO DO FOR VOMITING: The most common cause of vomiting is eating too much too quickly or eating something she shouldn't have. This is quite harmless, unless it becomes a frequent presentation; in other words, vomiting more than once a day or vomiting two or three days in a row calls for an in-depth review by your veterinarian. Other reasons dogs vomit usually concern illness, such as pancreatitis. Ask your veterinarian to run some tests, and then try to track down the answers. If your veterinarian can't find anything physically wrong, it may well be time to see a veterinary behaviorist or a certified dog behavior consultant. Some dogs become very possessive of their spastic regurgitations, and they think of this . . . er . . . output, as their property. Such dogs may do some resource guarding if you come between the dog and her slightly used meal, because the dog has every intention of re-eating these offerings rather rapidly.

Mealtime in the Multi-Dog Home

 My husband just brought home another dog. We already had two, and they're not exactly happy about it. Whenever we put the food bowls down, a fight ensues. Help!

 Of course they're not happy: two's company, but three's a pack! How would you like it if your husband brought home another wife and expected you to live with her? How happy would you be? You're going to have a problem unless you carefully integrate the dogs. I hope you introduced them on neutral territory outside the house, and your husband didn't come barging in the door with the new little interloper (that is, interloper from your other dogs' viewpoint)!

Be sure that only good things happen for your older dogs when the new one is around. Reward them for good behavior when they act nicely toward the newbie. And be sure everyone is polite and well mannered. Don't forget to train the newcomer and reinforce training with your older dogs. Make sure everyone is having a good time when they're together. Give them time apart and carefully monitor all interactions. And be sure that everyone has their own dish and can comfortably consume their own meals without worrying about having food stolen by the new kid in town.

Very young puppies will look for the best nipple to nurse from; in the same way, they will push each other out of the way to get to the food dish that's set up for the puppies when they're being weaned. Larger puppies can be a little pushier about making sure they get their fair share, but the breeder will watch to be sure that all puppies are eating enough and thriving. Birth order is unlikely to affect the way the dog eats when she arrives in your house. However, if you have an older, established dog at home, the house is her turf, and the baby will show deference to the older dog. It's also a good idea to train your dogs to Sit and wait politely until the dishes are down and then they can be told that it's okay to eat.

PART 5

PERSONALITY PROBLEMS

DOGS HAVE THEIR OWN UNIQUE

personalities, just as children do. Is it nature or nurture? It could be either or a combination of both. Each puppy in a litter has a different personality, which is why choosing a responsible breeder is so important if you decide to buy a puppy rather than adopt one from a shelter or a breed rescue organization. A good breeder knows the puppies so well that after getting to know you, he or she can tell which puppy will go well with your personality and lifestyle. A rescue dog, on the other hand, may come with baggage, so you'll have to figure out his particular puzzle as you try to resolve his personality issues.

For example, sometimes dogs are frightened by something in particular (as opposed to something in their past), and unless you can figure out what happens to trigger a specific reaction in your dog, you're going to have a difficult time resolving the issue.

When Your Dog Is a Wimp

If your dog hides from others—dogs or people—and acts afraid, including hiding behind your legs when someone approaches, you have a *fearful dog*. A fearful dog isn't happy. How can he be? The last time you felt afraid, were you happy about it?

 WHAT TO DO IF YOUR DOG IS A WIMP: If your dog is shy or fearful, he needs to have his confidence built slowly but surely. Get involved in an activity that will help build his confidence. One that I particularly like, because it's safe and you move at your own pace, is Canine Musical Freestyle. It's a choreographed dance routine to music with your dog, and it's appropriate for anyone. Go to the World Canine Freestyle Organization's website for more information, to watch videos, and to connect with Freestylers in your area: www.worldcaninefreestyle.org.

If dancing's not your thing, find other ways for your dog to meet all sorts of friendly people of all sizes, shapes, and colors, and see that he goes to lots of different fun places.

WHAT NOT TO DO IF YOUR DOG IS A WIMP: Don't put him into situations with aggressive dogs, which will make him feel defensive. Let him take his time and investigate. Don't tell him, "Oh, that's okay, Poopsie, that won't hurt you," because the message you're sending him is, "Uh, oh! Danger! Danger!" Just relax and let him find out for himself that the shopping cart isn't going to eat him alive, that the wall is just a wall, and so on. This is part of socialization, and he needs to learn that nearly everything in the world is normal. Don't do it all at once, though! That's called *flooding*— overwhelming your dog with too many new experiences at once—and it is very frightening for your dog. Do one new thing together every couple of days or so. You have a lifetime together, so there's no hurry and no need to overwhelm him.

Help for the Herder

My dog herds the kids, my husband, and even me, depending on what he seems to want and where he wants us to be. Why is he doing this, and how do we stop it?

Herding is a natural behavior for many dogs, such as the Bearded Collie, Border Collie, or Puli. It's a job they were born and bred to do. If they don't have other animals to herd, they'll tend to herd family members, gathering them together by walking behind them and in the case of some herding dogs, like Corgis, by nipping at their heels. In a case like this, this isn't biting behavior: it's normal herding behavior in certain breeds. You can try to distract the dog from this behavior by asking him to perform another task such as Sit or Down. But chances are, he won't be very happy about it if he has a strong herding instinct. You can't blame a dog for doing what he was born to do. Instead, get involved in a dog sport to keep your dog busy and active. You may want to seek out Herding Trials in your area so that your dog can have fun doing what he does best. Contact the American Kennel Club (www.akc.org) for information about Herding Clinics and Herding Trials in your area.

In the future, if you don't want this type of behavior, don't get a herding breed. Also avoid a mixed-breed dog who may have a herding breed in him, because that behavior may surface.

Getting to Know Your Breed

To prevent—or at least to understand—potential doggie problems, learn as much about your dog's particular breed or breed group or type as possible. Some general examples:

- **Terriers** are feisty, fun, and intelligent. Their intelligence is often mistaken for stubbornness, a trait for which they've gotten a bad rap over the years. The problem, of course, is that most Terriers are bored. If he has done something once, why should he do it the same way again? Make life more interesting for him and know that your training will have to have some variation so that it's like a game.

- **Herding dogs** will do just that: they herd family members if they don't have a job to do. If you're determined to have one of these breeds, like a Collie, German Shepherd, Corgi, Shetland Sheepdog, or Puli, remember that they will herd the other animals in the house, and if there aren't any, prepare for them to herd the humans, with some of the breeds nipping at your heels. That's pure instinct, bred into them over the years. Getting involved in a dog sport will keep your dog busy and active.

- **Working dogs** encompass a number of breeds including the Rottweiler, Doberman Pinscher, and Black Russian Terrier. These dogs are born and bred to work. They're hardwired to work. They need early, gentle training to channel that work ethic in the right direction. Without proper training, you might just as well have a loaded rifle lying around your house. All these dogs can be wonderful companions, but whether or not they end up being wonderful depends, as with every breed, on you. Knowing that the dog has a strong work ethic will help you to appropriately channel his energy into a sport or other activity that will work his mind and body.

- **Hounds** come in two varieties: *Sighthounds* are those bred to hunt by sight, and *Scenthounds* are those bred to sniff the ground and air to look for their prey. Sighthounds tend to run like the wind, and then want to lie on the sofa. Scenthounds prefer to sniff everything, so walks will always involve time to stop and smell the flowers. Training them for Variable Surface Tracking will be fun for the dog—go to AKC's website for information at www.akc.org. (Variable Surface Tracking is not the same as training to be a Search and Rescue, or SAR, dog, which is a job for professionals. The owners need to know CPR and other emergency medical skills in case they find the person alive, and they need to be prepared to find dead bodies and help their dogs cope with the stress of that sort of find. Scenthounds are not the only dogs who do a good job at SAR work; other breeds, like the Beauceron, are excellent SAR dogs but not necessarily the housedog of your dreams.)

- **Sporting dogs** love water and running in fields. Among these active dogs are the Golden Retriever, Labrador Retriever, Pointers, Cocker Spaniels, and Irish Setters. You have to make time for such activities, which means you have to enjoy them. The way the dog responds to each activity will help you train your dog so playtime is natural and fun. What's really a "bonus" about clicker training is that, using the clicker, you can mark or capture a behavior that you like and channel the dog's natural instincts into something productive and fun.

It's very easy to train Sporting dogs to retrieve, for example, with clicker training. You certainly don't need choke collars and those awful ear pinches to accomplish your goal!

- **Non-sporting dogs** provide an interesting array, from the Dalmatian who is a pretty tough working dog (and not the cutesy little canine of cartoon fame) to the fluffy, sweet, and funny Bichon Frisé, who will turn in an Oscar-worthy performance just to get your attention. This group of dogs is so diverse that it's rather like a catch-all category for a number of breeds that also includes the Boston Terrier, Keeshond, Shiba Inu, and Lhasa Apso. Could these dogs be in other groups? Sure! The Lowchen, for example, is a Toy dog everywhere else in the world but is in the AKC's Non-Sporting Group. Schipperkes were herding dogs before becoming known as Barge Dogs in Belgium. Non-Sporting Group has become something of a catch-all for a range of dog breeds, and many of them would be found in a different group outside the United States or the American Kennel Club's registry. Actually, the AKC has seven groups in all.

- **Toy dogs** are all bred to be companions, and even in that group you'll find some of the breeds in other groups in other countries. For example, the Shih Tzu is only a Toy in the United States, Canada, and Bermuda. If you were to go to the United Kingdom, for example, you would find that breed in the Utility Group. These dogs, too, will have fun doing dog sports like Rally-O, which is a fun sort of obedience course with signs along the way where to stop and perform the specified behavior.

Mama's Little Helper

"I have four Cardigan Corgis. My old girl, Tansy, is eleven-and-a-half years old and is queen of the house. The other three are outside most of the day and come in the house in the evenings. When it's time to go back out, they sometimes act like they have never heard the word 'outside' before. They just stand there. It's at this point that Tansy will get out of her chair and proceed to go

> outside. Of course, the others then decide to fol-
> low her out. As soon as all three are outside, Tansy
> will immediately turn around and come back in.
> Then I get this look that says, 'What's so hard
> about that?' I call her the Judas goat. " —Zoë

This isn't as mysterious as it sounds. Corgis are herding dogs—they were bred specifically to herd other animals. In fact, without other animals to herd, they'll herd their owners, the children, the cat, or whoever else is available—kind of the canine version of *Born to Boogie*. So, the escort service provided by Tansy is very much in keeping with her breed. This is one reason it's important to know what you want in a dog before you get it. Each breed was born to do something, and you want be sure it's something you can live with throughout the dog's life.

TOP 10 MOST ANNOYING BEHAVIOR: **Separation Anxiety**

For many owners and their dogs, separation anxiety is a very serious problem. It's better, of course, if it never starts, but if it does, you have to address the issue.

Remember that there's a big difference between boredom and separation anxiety. A dog with separation anxiety cannot bear to have you out of his sight for a minute. You go off to work, and he destroys the house in his effort to get to you. You'll see the teeth marks around windowsills and frames pulled away. I once saw a toilet half pulled out of a nearly destroyed downstairs bathroom.

A bored dog might do some inappropriate chewing or pull something off the bed or chairs. The dog with separation anxiety will actually try to escape the house, which is why the damage is so much more than that caused by boredom.

WHAT TO DO FOR SEPARATION ANXIETY: Dogs need to learn, from the time that they're young, that they can't be with you all the time—and that's okay, because you'll always return. Start by putting him in the crate for a few minutes, with the door closed, while you're in the room. Don't open the door if he protests; only open it when he's quiet. He'll soon get the idea that it's okay to be alone for a bit. Leave the house for a few minutes when he's in a safe place with the radio or television turned on and toys to amuse himself. Be sure that he knows you will always return. Don't make a big fuss. Be very matter-of-fact about it. Gradually extend the time you are away by a minute or two every day or so. He'll learn that you can be out of his sight and things will be just fine; he's not "an abandoned child"!

When you do leave, always turn the radio or television on so he'll have the sound of human voices. Give him a special puzzle toy to play with or a hollow toy stuffed with a biscuit or smeared inside with flavored doggy toothpaste or peanut butter. Leave his crate door open with a soft cuddly pad inside and a favorite toy to cuddle with for a nap. Be sure a puppy has a separate potty area if someone can't get home at lunchtime to walk him.

When Your House Is One Big Chew Toy

You come home from work and discover that your puppy has been teething on the legs of your coffee table—those telltale tiny tooth marks are quite evident. Or your adult dog has been adding his own decorations to the windowsills. Why?

All dogs chew. It's what they do for a range of reasons, but mostly, puppies do it when they're teething, because just like human babies, their gums are itchy and they need to relieve that itch. If there's nothing more appealing available, your puppy is likely to find something like a chair leg or anything else within reach, which may include your favorite pair of shoes, the handle of your best purse, your favorite belt, and so on. Puppies and adult dogs should be provided with a range of toys to choose from, including soft, harder (not too hard, though, because you don't want your puppy or adult dog to fracture a tooth), and something sort of in between. Let your canine family member choose what type of toy he wants at a particular time.

Be thoughtful about the shape of the toys. Some have little nubby pieces on them that are meant to massage the gums. Others are soft; still others might squeak. (Don't, however, choose a toy that's shaped like a shoe or give your pup an old shoe of your own to chew on. He's not going to understand why it's okay to chew that and not your new Bruno Magli loafers or Manolo Blahnik heels. A shoe is a shoe is a shoe.) Another good choice is one of the specifically designed hollowed-out toys. You can put a biscuit inside, or you can smear the inside with flavored doggie toothpaste or a thin coating of peanut butter. Such toys will keep him occupied for a long time while you're out of the house, and he can happily chew on the toy as well as enjoy what's inside. Wash this type of toy out before you use it again if you've used a filling other than a biscuit.

Never let your puppy chew on your fingers. If he does, yelp as a littermate would, and replace your hand or fingers with an appropriate toy. Don't let your puppy play with your hands because you want to reinforce *bite inhibition* in your puppy (not biting down hard); he needs to know that biting a human isn't ever to be accepted. Give him an acceptable behavior to perform instead, and then praise him when he does it.

Puppy Proofing 101

To make sure your dog isn't chewing on anything dangerous, get down and look at your house from a dog's perspective.

1. Pick up all small objects from the floor. This includes small toys, hairpins, thumbtacks, needles, pins, and so on.
2. Put locks on all cabinet doors. An inquisitive dog or puppy can easily get at hazardous household chemicals, such as detergent or bleach.
3. Tape electrical cords to the wall. A teething puppy or dog can easily electrocute himself by chewing on one.
4. Buy and use covers for unused electrical outlets.
5. Leave the toilet seat down—drinking from the toilet bowl can be hazardous to your dog's health, and a puppy could accidentally fall in. It's also poisonous if you use one of those cleaners that works every time you flush.

Retrievers are considered especially *mouthy* as puppies, and they usually have a *soft mouth,* which means they hold things—like fingers—gently. It's fairly easy to teach them helpful behaviors like Trade You (see Part 1). Most Terriers, on the other hand, like to hold on to things tenaciously, and they, along with all dogs, have an *opposition reflex* (that is, you pull one way, they pull the other). This is why teaching Trade You, even to dogs who hang on tight to what's in their mouths, is very important.

Tug-of-War . . . or Not?

Some people like to play tug-of-war with their dogs; this can be bad for some dogs and okay for others. To play tug-of-war, you must control the game and you must win; otherwise, the dog will learn that he can take things away from you or anyone else, which will make him pushy (exactly the kind of dog you don't want). Keep in mind that the smallest dogs can be hurt badly if swung around on the end of a tug toy, and their teeth can be pulled out of alignment playing this "game." Think before you initiate a game of tug-of-war.

Digging

Although most dogs find great satisfaction from digging, you may not be happy if your dog decides to exhume the bulbs you've just planted or makes your lawn look like a mine field.

WHAT TO DO FOR A DIGGER: In order to save your lawn and flowers and make your dog happy, here's a wonderful compromise: choose one area of your yard that's just for your dog's digging pleasure. Teach him to use it by burying a toy and letting him "find it" a few times. Soon he'll learn, as you praise him, that this is a good place to dig, because he never knows what he may find! You, your garden, and your dog will be supremely happy.

Most Annoying Behavior: **Thunder Phobia**

Fear of thunder and thunderstorms is fairly common. Some dogs become so fearful that they will break through doors in an effort to escape the frightening sound, while other dogs aren't bothered by thunder. For the owner of the phobic dog, it can be a very distressing situation. Not only thunder but fireworks, gunshots, acorns falling on the roof, and so on can trigger the fearful reaction. Interestingly, as I write this, a new study of fear and thunder phobia is in the planning stages and should be under way by the time you read this. The investigators want to try to determine whether this is a hereditary condition.

 WHAT TO DO FOR THUNDER PHOBIA: Some veterinary behaviorists prescribe medication, but this need not be the first thing you try. There are CDs of thunder to help condition your dog to the sound, but they're not precisely accurate—canine hearing is so acute that the dog can usually tell the difference between real and recorded thunder. One thing that helps the dog feel calmer, along with your calm demeanor, is an anxiety wrap or a tightly fitting T-shirt to make him feel more secure, like a baby in swaddling clothing. If the anxiety wrap or T-shirt doesn't help, seek the help of a professional behavior consultant. Even if the dog is put on medication, you will still need to implement a behavior-modification program, which may include a recording of thunder to help desensitize your dog. There has been some talk about using melatonin supplements to help treat thunder phobia, but if you are going to try it, you will need to talk to your veterinarian about both dosage and brand because some of the over-the-counter "remedies" can be mixed with other ingredients that can be unsafe for canine consumption. Only your veterinarian can make that determination. Other people use flower essence products. Do they work? Good question! Perhaps if the owner thinks it works, the owner is calmer and that helps the dog to calm down. Or, perhaps, the flower essences do work. Frankly, at this point, the jury is still out.

 WHAT NOT TO DO FOR THUNDER PHOBIA: Don't tell your dog (perhaps in baby talk), "It's okay, it's just thunder," because your dog isn't going to believe you. And don't totally ignore the problem. You can find help, but it's a matter of discovering the right thing for your dog. Don't leave the dog alone if there's a storm expected. If you have to be away from the house, be sure your dog has a "safe" place to go. His crate can be ideal. Leave the door open but drape something over the opening on the sides so he'll feel secure. When you come home, you can put on some gentle music. Sue Raimond, a pioneer in harp therapy, has created harp music just for calming animals. While attending one of her lectures, I nearly fell asleep and thought about buying some of her music for my own stressful days!

OCD—The Obsessive-Compulsive Doggie

When you see a dog licking endlessly and it's not an allergy, or you see him repeatedly spinning and seriously trying to catch his tail, fence running, pacing, and demonstrating pica (eating things like rocks), you may be seeing signs of OCD—obsessive-compulsive disorder. Research is showing that the condition appears to be genetic and is more common in some breeds of dogs than others. When an older dog chews too much, this can also be a sign of OCD.

 WHAT TO DO FOR OCD: If you see any of the signs of OCD, take your dog to a veterinarian, who may recommend a consultation with a veterinary behaviorist or a Ph.D.-level behaviorist. Treatment consists of behavior modification, along with medication (usually an antidepressant)

to help manage the problem. There is no cure, as of this writing, but the problem can be managed. Most of the dogs with OCD are male and along with mixed breeds, you'll be likely to find OCD, when it occurs, in such breeds as German Shepherds, Dalmatians, Bulldogs, and Rottweilers, but this doesn't preclude the problem occurring in other breeds. Interestingly, the dogs who are most likely to chase their tails are the ones who herd.

You'll usually begin to be aware of OCD when your dog reaches adolescence. Ahhh, those teen years. In an OCD study at the University of Pennsylvania, many of the animals also had other behavior issues like separation anxiety or attention-seeking, and they tended to practice their OCD behaviors in private.

PART 6

SEX AND THE DOG OWNER

DOGS CAN BE REALLY FUNNY OR

interesting (you can choose your own euphemism!) when it comes to their humans and s-e-x. People who have children often complain that they have to schedule sex so the kids don't interrupt. The dog owner is in pretty much the same leaky boat and rowing as fast as he or she can! If maintaining a relationship with the opposite sex isn't difficult enough, it can get even more complicated when you add a canine to the equation. Over the years, I have been surprised when people have called on me to solve problems with their dogs ranging from "My dog doesn't like my girlfriend," to "My dog watches us have sex." The answers are different depending, of course, on the dog and the others involved, but believe me, the questions are always interesting.

Dinner Discourse

"My husband has a friend who completed his priestship for the Anglican Church. We invited him to join us for Christmas dinner with a group of our friends who we refer to as 'our dysfunctional family.' He accepted.

While we were finishing our drinks, one of the women asked me what I had decided about breeding my Rhodesian Ridgeback, Stormy. I told her that, at that time, the only thing I knew for certain, besides that I was planning to breed her on her next season, was that I was *not* going to do an AI (artificial insemination). Then, of course, she wanted to know why I arrived at that decision. I explained that a breeder with many years of experience told me it was not such a good idea on a virgin bitch. Of course, all Father Albert heard of this conversation was the last two words—'virgin bitch.' We could have done a MasterCard commercial with the look on his face as the 'priceless' part. So I then had to explain to him what the beginning of our conversation had been. He looked at me with a strange look as I began and said, 'I'm certain *this* is the first time I have *ever* heard those two words used next to each other in a sentence!'

We're still good friends, and he has since learned more than he ever wanted to know about dog breeding. " —Anne

MOST ANNOYING BEHAVIOR: **The Sex Police**

A syndicated newspaper columnist called me one day to help her respond to a reader's question. The woman and her husband couldn't have sex without the dog staring at them. It was very disconcerting for the couple and was turning out to be the ultimate form of birth control. What could they do?

I've lost count of how many people have told me that their dogs act as the sex police. No one of the opposite sex can get near them because the dog will snarl, bark, growl, and so on. Even cuddling or trying to touch the other person is off-limits in the dog's estimation. One woman proudly showed me how her tiny dog would snarl at her husband whenever he approached her while the dog was in her arms. They laughed. Big mistake. Laughing only reinforces bad behavior, because the dog interprets the laughing as approval. Most owners think that resource guarding concerns only food, toys, or some other object that the dog has acquired. They don't think of themselves as a resource for the dog. See Part 3 for details on resource guarding.

WHAT TO DO IF YOUR DOG ACTS AS THE SEX POLICE: This type of resource guarding is an aggression problem (see Part 3). If this happens, have the person she's guarding (you, if it's you) distract her with alternate behaviors and reward her for them. Give her puzzle toys and click and treat for good behavior. The times that she's calm while you and your significant other are cuddling, you can tell her she's being good. If you can plan ahead, you can take her for a walk or practice her particular dog sport just before your cuddle time, so that she will be tired enough to settle down with a chew toy or for a nap.

 WHAT NOT TO DO IF YOUR DOG ACTS AS THE SEX POLICE: Don't laugh because it will only reinforce bad behavior. And don't yell at her. That will only confuse and upset your dog and make the situation worse.

When Your Dog Doesn't Like Your Significant Other

We share a special relationship with our dogs, and they with us, but they can also impact our relationships with other people. Personally, I don't especially trust anyone who doesn't like animals. This doesn't mean that all animal lovers are wonderful people, but if your dog indicates that she doesn't like someone, consider yourself warned about that person's character. I always relied on my dog to let me know what kind of guy I was dating. If he passed the dog's inspection, he was an okay guy. However, if the dog didn't like him, I knew there was something wrong, even if the guy was pretending to like the dog.

Dogs cut right through that façade. They know when someone's real, phony, nasty, and so on. And I'm not the only person who has noticed this canine ability! I've often thought that there would be an interesting business in renting out dogs to inspect prospective dates.

 WHAT TO DO WHEN YOUR DOG DOESN'T LIKE YOUR SIGNIFICANT OTHER: If you want your dog and your significant other to share a better relationship, and your significant other is willing, try to set up some bonding time and fun things they can do together. Let the other person feed the dog when visiting, play games, and give treat rewards. Always give your dog attention when the other person is there, so that your dog doesn't view the new human as a rival for your affection and attention. Try to behave as normally as possible and be inclusive.

 WHAT NOT TO DO WHEN YOUR DOG DOESN'T LIKE YOUR SIGNIFICANT OTHER: As tempting as it may be, don't immediately throw the guy out of the door and tell him that you're sorry you can't see him anymore because your dog doesn't approve. Give him a chance to prove whether the dog's right. And don't yell at your dog. That will only add fuel to the fire. Also don't put the dog in another room; that's not the way to build a relationship, and it certainly won't give the dog and your significant other an opportunity to bond.

Two's Company;
Three's a Canine Chaperone

"When I was single and in my twenties, I dated often. Since I had my own place and lived alone with my Doberman, Duke, I usually did not let men into my home. The day finally came when I had to ask a guy in whom I had dated for a while. We were getting very serious and were on the verge of getting engaged. John was a macho construction worker and had the typical 'I'm a man' attitude. But inside, he was a marshmallow.

We sat down together on the couch in the living room to watch TV. He put his arm around me and started to kiss me. He got a little bit carried away, but nothing serious. I told him to stop, but he did not believe me. I told him a second time to behave himself. I did not go beyond kissing before marriage. Finally, I told him that if he did not act like a gentleman, he was going to get hurt. He laughed, since he's bigger and stronger than I am. We sat for a while and watched TV, and then he started to kiss me again. Not wanting things to get out of hand, I warned him again and he, joking, said, 'You and what army?' I looked at Duke, who was lying nearby watching, and gave him his command, 'Watch!' He immediately jumped up, came over, and sat right in front of John on full alert. Duke understood exactly what was going on and what I wanted. What I failed to tell John was that Duke was a fully trained personal protection dog.

John was a perfect gentleman from that point on. If he so much as moved an arm in my direction, Duke showed him his pearly whites. What amazed me was John's good nature about all of this. We did get married, and Duke remained my protector for the rest of his life.

Good thing for John that I never gave Duke his 'Nixon' command—the groin attack. Maybe it was a good thing for me, too. **"** —Sherry

Playing Second Fiddle to Fido

When my wife and I got married, she had a dog who went everywhere with her. I like dogs, don't get me wrong, but the dog gets fed before I do and he still goes pretty much everywhere we go. When we watch television, he's right there, sitting between us, and she coos to him as if he were a baby. He even sleeps with us. Enough is enough. I could swear she loves that dog more than she loves me!

Surely you were aware of your wife's relationship with her dog before you were married. Did you

think that would magically change once the vows were exchanged? She wasn't exchanging the dog for you, she was adding you to her family, and you were adding her (and her dog!) to yours. Have you discussed this with her?

Who feeds the dog? Who gives the dog water? If your wife currently does, try assuming some of the dog-care responsibilities so you can be the source of good things and he becomes more bonded to you.

You also might get involved in a dog sport with him, with your wife's blessing. Remember that this has always been her dog. Suggest that you do things without the dog, too. Plan a romantic evening just for you two. Tell her this isn't the night for "children," it's just for the "grown-ups." For those special nights, you might buy the dog a special bed that is placed in another room and a special doggy puzzle toy to keep him occupied while you and your wife are . . . er . . . occupied, too.

Don't yell at the dog to get away, and don't yell at your wife unless you want to be a new contestant on *Divorce Court*. The way to your wife's heart is obviously through her dog, so I hope you haven't been only pretending to like him. And don't give your wife an ultimatum. If you tell her that either the dog goes or you go, it's going to be a pretty easy decision, so you might start looking for an apartment of your own if that's what you have in mind.

The French-Kissing Dog

 My dog Spicy excitedly greets people by cleaning out their tonsils with her tongue. For some odd reason, this does not go over as intended with my boyfriend. Spicy *really* doesn't understand why this gesture of affection is so unappreciated. She is, after all, an expert providing service for free. Should I tell my boyfriend to lighten up?

 Teach your dog to act politely when guests arrive by telling her to Sit. Tell your guests in advance not to pet your dog if she jumps up on them because you need their help in teaching her to behave in an acceptable manner. In fact, you can invite friends over to help you with this; you practice going to the door with your dog and having her sit when you open the door, and then the person greets you and pats the dog. Be sure to teach your dog an alternate behavior like Sit because she can't jump up and kiss if she has just been told Sit.

Also, if you allow her to French kiss you, she's going to do the same to your guests. How can she tell that you like it but they don't? Some people enjoy a doggy kiss (minus the tonsil cleaning, thank you very much), while others don't like any sort of kissing from canines. The kissing behavior has been said to have its roots in feeding behavior: puppies lick the food from their mother's face. Whatever the roots may be, many of us can think of nothing nicer than doggie kisses and nothing smells as sweet to many of us as puppy breath. (The source of that sweet smell, by the way, is supposed to be broken capillaries from new teeth breaking through.) Many dogs can discern the difference between people who like kisses and those who don't, while others are so happy-go-lucky that they don't bother with the niceties of reading body language. If your guests don't like to be kissed, you can teach your dog to shake hands instead.

Don't coo to your boyfriend, "Ooooh, he wuvs you!" Nor should you yell at your dog. If you're aware of this sort of greeting behavior, warn your boyfriend in advance and enlist his help. Tell him not to scream, yell, or push the dog away, but to simply ignore the behavior or tell the dog to Sit. This can be rewarded with a tasty treat that you give to your boyfriend to present to the dog. Screaming and yelling will only frighten the dog and can cause behavior problems later. She will not be as inclined to like people after a very bad experience with a human.

Loving a Dog Is a Many-Splendored Thing

"I had just started dating this really beautiful girl. She was smart, funny, and fun to be around. She invited me back to her place. I accepted the invitation, especially since she said she wanted me to meet her dog. I love dogs. But waiting for her inside the door was one of those little dogs. I thought she had a dog, not an animated bed slipper. Worse, she picked him up and kissed him on the lips! Oh yuck! That just made me nauseated."

—Fred

Dogs come in more sizes than any other species, so it's hard to understand why anyone would assume that the dog was large (and you do know what they say about the word "assume"). I think you can avoid surprises by asking what kind of dog a person has, how big it is, and whether it's a mixed breed or a breed name you don't recognize. That, at least, will give you a clue about the dog's size. And it will show that you're interested in the other person's dog. Get to know the dog before you decide whether you like her instead of having a preconceived notion. Little dogs *are* real dogs. They're just smaller. And all dogs can be taught that kissing is unacceptable behavior, but if it's someone else's dog and she enjoys it, you'll either have to get used to it or find another woman to date.

Don't refer to her beloved companion as a "drop-kick dog," "barking bed slipper," or any other epithet unless you never want to see that girl again. If you don't like to have dogs kiss you, be honest, but don't be nasty about it. And if you're so concerned about size, you have a problem that I can't solve.

Frankly, I've dealt with this situation up close and personal. I've never had a problem kissing dogs on the lips or having them kiss me. My mother used to tell me that no man would want to kiss me if he saw me kissing the dog. I pointed out that I wouldn't be interested in any man who didn't understand that I kiss the dog. And, to be perfectly blunt, dear reader, some of the men who've kissed me could have taken lessons from the dog!

🐾

Bedtime in the Multi-Dog Home

Have you ever tried sharing a full-size bed with six dogs? It's kind of like playing an odd game of Twister. For those dog owners who haven't yet invested in a king-size bed, there are some things you can do to get a good night's rest without asking your human bedmate to curl up his or her feet so your dog can be more comfortable.

 WHAT TO DO WHEN YOU HAVE MORE THAN ONE DOG: If you have more than one dog, you can rotate them so one of them gets to sleep with you on certain nights while the others can sleep with you on other nights. Meanwhile, have an assortment of crates and dog beds as an alternative for those who won't be joining you in bed. Or you could do the opposite and choose not to let any dog sleep with you. Just be sure that each dog has a comfortable bed of her own. It's important to note that letting your dog sleep with you will not spoil the dog. If you and the dog(s) enjoy it, there's no reason to stop. But sleeping with you is a privilege that that can be revoked for bad behavior, and permission won't be restored until the behavior problem has been resolved. Never yell at the dog or pull or push her off the bed. She should be well trained enough for you to say "Off," if sleeping with you isn't allowed.

If your dog would prefer a bed of her own in your room, there are plenty of beds available in various price ranges, from a basic low-cost mat to an elaborate decorator design that costs nearly a king's ransom. When your dog is older and can't get into your bed by herself, you can either pile up pillows near your bed or buy special doggy stairs to put next to the bed. You can also move those steps to help your dog get into the car. If your dog becomes arthritic, there are special mattresses to help her achy joints, and there are beds made for dogs who become incontinent. That's probably when you won't want to share your bed with her. Alas, no one wants to sleep with a bed wetter.

PART 7

GOODWILL ON THE GO

DOGS ARE GLORIOUS CREATURES AND

wonderful friends. But they have to learn to live within the community. If they behave in a manner that's acceptable to others, there's no reason why they can't travel with you, hang out with your friends, go to work with you if your company allows it, and so on. Without proper manners, however, there isn't a whole lot of difference between a dog and your shiftless brother-in-law eating your food, lying on your sofa watching TV, and farting. Both would have the same . . . er . . . charming appeal. That is to say, none, although the dog might be more grateful for the place to crash and would probably be more affectionate.

After you've gotten past all the basic stuff like house-training and teaching your dog to Sit, Stay, Come, Wait, and walk nicely on a leash, you'll have a companion who can be taken to public places where dogs are allowed.

Plane, train, automobile, or even the ferry, your dog should learn to travel in a crate or carrier. A smaller dog can often travel onboard the plane with you, provided he weighs less than twenty-one pounds and his carrier fits under the seat. A secure crate in the car will also be a safe haven in case you have to stop short or if there's an accident. Larger dogs, such as guide dogs, are often taught to lie on the floor of the car for safety, but a crate is optimum.

Checklist for Travelers

When traveling with your dog, it's best to be prepared for an emergency. And, if Murphy's Law prevails, when you have these items, you'll never need them:

- A first-aid kit for your dog (make one yourself or buy one that is made and prepacked especially for dogs). If you're making your own you'll want to have roll cotton, cotton balls, gauze pads and gauze tape, hydrogen peroxide (be sure to check the expiration date so you always have a fresh bottle), vet wrap, antibiotic ointment, hydrocortisone ointment, scissors, eyewash, tweezers, silver nitrate, a thermometer, oral syringe, one-inch white tape, an emergency ice pack, a magnifying glass, a flashlight or penlight, and aspirin (but know the correct dosage before you give it to your dog!). You may want to add an electrolyte fluid, a meat-based baby food, a large towel, and exam gloves.

- A current photo of your dog in case he gets loose
- Your veterinarian's phone number
- A collar or harness and leash with a detailed tag
- Microchip your dog (and register the microchip for positive identification in case he gets lost)
- Plastic bags (and perhaps a pooper scooper for big dogs) for cleanup
- Toys and a crate for travel
- Some of your dog's regular food
- Bottled water and water dish for your dog to prevent diarrhea

Traveling with your four-legged best friend can be the best fun you can have. Just be sure everyone is safe.

Dogs at 30,000 Feet

Plane travel brings up two options. The small dog can go on board with you unless you're flying overseas, in which case he'll have to go in the cargo hold, and all medium, large, and giant dogs always go in the cargo hold. And, yes, you pay extra either way. No one has ever been able to explain to me why a carry-on is free if there's a laptop computer in it but it's not free if it's a laptop dog! As far as I know, there's no rule saying that the airlines have to charge extra to the customer who is losing legroom by having their dog under the seat and not bothering anyone else. But they do.

If the dog has to go in the cargo hold, be sure the airline knows that you have a dog there and that the cargo compartment is pressurized and not cold. Those are important points if your dog is going to survive the journey. Be certain to have plenty of identification on the dog as well as on the crate and bungee the door closed so it won't pop open, allowing your dog to escape. Your dog should respond to the words Sit and Stay no matter who utters them, or your dog may not survive the trip. Tie a plastic bag of extra food to the crate in case the trip takes longer than anticipated.

Air Travel Tips

A frequent doggie traveler offers this wonderful advice: "When traveling with a dog on an airplane. I always print out a page with a favorite picture and a standard statement under the picture:

"Hi! My name is [insert dog's name]. I'm a/an [insert breed or mix], and I am on my way to a show [or wherever else] with my mom! She is flying in seat number [insert number]. Both she and I are nervous about my flying. Please call me by my name, as it reassures me and eases my fears. If you would, please ask the pilot to let my mom know I am on board. Thanks for taking good care of me, and please don't open my door, as I might be afraid and would run. I won't bite but would lick you to death.'

"I also take a 5 x 8 picture on board with me with an added area at the bottom and hand it to the flight attendants to give/show to the pilot as I enter: 'Hi! My name is [insert dog's name], and I am traveling below in the cargo hold. While I am a show dog [delete if not appropriate], I am a very much loved pet to my mom who is in seat number [insert number]. Would you please make sure I am loaded and secure, and then let my mom know before we pull away to leave? Thanks!'

"The crews always love this. They have told me they like knowing about their 'precious' cargo, why the dog is traveling, where it is going, and a bit about the dog, too!"

This is excellent advice whether your dog is going to a show or on vacation, or you're moving to a new home in another place and flying out there with your dog. Just fill in the blanks with your specific information.

 WHAT TO DO WHEN FLYING: Along with being sure the dog is okay on the day you travel, be certain to get him accustomed to his crate or carrier long before you leave on your trip. If he's going on board, in your pretravel training, keep his carrier near your feet with the door open so he can get used to the idea that he will be near your feet. Close it with him inside for a few minutes, extending the time just a little bit more each day. He'll have to learn to stay in his carrier for the duration of the flight. And be sure to walk him before you board the flight (or before your dog is put in his crate for the trip) and upon arrival. If necessary bring Wee-Wee Pads with you and take your dog into the restroom and allow him to relieve himself on the pad. Put the soiled pad in a plastic bag and dispose of it in the trash just like a used diaper. Travel with paper towels and plastic bags so that you can clean up after your dog, and also take your dog's food and bottled water, which you now have to buy after you've cleared security. Otherwise, you can pack a bottle or two in your suitcase and purchase more when you reach your destination. Water changes from place to place, and you don't want to upset your dog's digestive tract. Take a first-aid kit along for emergencies as well as a photo of your dog in case he gets lost.

 WHAT NOT TO DO WHEN FLYING: Do not tranquilize the dog before you fly, because the tranquilizer can drop the dog's blood pressure and slow his responses. He really doesn't need sedation. He just needs to learn, as with everything else, that travel is a normal experience. Don't worry, most dogs take advantage of their time in the carrier and nap. Don't leave his excrement for others to step in when you walk him. Clean it up!

Car Travel

There are some rules of the road to follow when your dog is in the car. First, depending upon his size, he should either be crated, wearing a seatbelt, or in a doggie car seat for his safety and yours. Don't let him jump over the seat, off and on your lap, or roam around the foot pedals. This can result in an accident. Please don't let him hang his head out the window. There are all kinds of things flying through the air, like debris from the car or truck in front of you. If that gets into his eyes or ears, rest assured you'll have a veterinary bill in your future. If you have to stop suddenly, your dog will go flying through the car or the window itself if he isn't properly placed in the car in a safe place.

If you're driving, plan pit stops for the dog as well as yourself. If you have to "go," your dog does, too. It's a good idea anyway to get out and stretch every three or four hours—more often if you have a bad back or circulation problems in your legs. Walking your dog will help both of you. Just plan the extra time when you're arranging your trip.

If your dog gets carsick, you can try giving him gingersnaps. You can also put him in a car seat or fasten him in with a doggy seatbelt if he's larger, so that he can see out the window. It can be rather like a seasick person on a cruise ship who needs to see the horizon.

The Car Pool

"After our local dog show, people were leaving the air-conditioned civic center and heading for home. Mind you, this was after getting very little sleep, sharing our house with three additional women and twelve additional Basset Hounds for the weekend, assisting the announcer, leading a couple of guided tours of the shows, and stewarding in the obedience ring for two shows and a match. My sweet and loving wife (alias Crazy Basset Lady) turned to me and innocently asked, 'Would you mind running the dogs home in the car?' I should have realized she was speaking literally. 'The dogs' consisted of our three girls and a friend's six dogs (three girls and three boys). 'The car' was our '92 Mitsubishi Mirage hatchback. Did I mention that one of the girls was in heat and wearing panties? How about the boy, Abel, riding shotgun? A young gun-slinging red and white looking to meet the new school marm or any of the other five girls. The other 'boyz in the hood' were pups. Uh, huh! Well, does that set the stage for our fifteen-mile drive? Not quite. Of course, there is the ninety-degree temperature with high humidity and no AC in the car! Yes?

I drove into the arena to get them. Everyone stopped packing up to watch the three women load Basset after Basset into the back of the little car. We took off to a round of applause, with yours truly feeling like the driver of the clown car at the circus. Before we got very far *someone* ripped the panties off the girl du jour. Fortunately—or not—I had Mr. Testosterone as copilot. . . . I'd been wishing for God as copilot. I was sure God wouldn't be whining and trying to push his nose into my ear to talk about the good-looking passengers.

The back of the car was divided by a barrier of sorts and for those areas uncovered 100 percent by the barrier, an elastic net was strung. I proceeded down the highway, drawing stares from the Sunday traffic. As you might have guessed, by about halfway, the dogs organized a breakout.

Heads poked around the net to the right and left. With Abel riding shotgun, his window was raised enough to deter further banditry. My left elbow became busy holding the heads back. While under attack, I was forced to clear space, and then further close the window to prevent the troops from bailing out. While busy protecting my flanks, 'the boyz' leapt up and unhooked the elastic cargo net, and the girls tried oozing over the top of the barrier. After gaining temporary safety along my flanks, I flashed my right arm up across the headrests, adding to the barrier. I stopped the charge, but took a number of slobber hits along the arm.

Driving the last three miles or so, I carefully focused my attention and managed to arrive in one piece. I was never so glad to see home and know now how Bilbo Baggins must have felt after venturing off with his own troop of dwarves. I didn't end up with a magic ring, but I still had my Grounds Chairman badge securely pinned to my shirt! **"** —Bob

Ah, yes, Bob proves the old saying that no good deed shall go unpunished. Dogs will be dogs, and a testosterone-crazed male in a small space with a bitch in heat is just too much of a temptation. Driving with nine uncrated dogs under the circumstances is either an incredibly brave or foolish thing to do. Probably both. Thankfully, Bob was able to maintain his sense of humor, which is, no doubt, a saving grace.

Take Your Dog to Work Day

An annual June event, Take Your Dog to Work Day is a wonderful idea. Pet Sitters International (PSI) is a driving force behind this special day. It also serves as a promotion to encourage people to adopt a dog from a shelter. Other groups have joined with PSI to help promote the special day. It's estimated that as many as ten thousand companies in the United States and Canada have participated. Dogs are great at destressing their human friends and acquaintances. In order to take your dog to the office, you have to be certain that your dog is friendly toward both people and other animals, that he is housetrained, that you can keep him in a secure area near your desk (perhaps in an exercise pen or a baby gate), and that you can take breaks and walk him. Also be sure he has food and water, a pad to lie on, and some toys to play with. Make sure your dog is not an excessive barker, and ask a coworker to watch your dog if you have to be away from your desk for any length of time. Most important: make sure your company's owner wants to participate before you simply waltz in with your dog.

The Office "Critic"

"I took my Border Collie, Einstein, to work with me one Sunday afternoon. Yes, I had to work on a Sunday. He's housetrained, but you never know when he'll decide to leave someone a 'present.' As usual, I checked the floor for Einstein 'pressies' before we left on Sunday night. But on Monday morning, I was informed that Einstein the Genius was banned from work, as he had left a present in the boardroom—and would I go and clean it up?" —Samantha

WHAT TO DO IF YOUR DOG MISBEHAVES AT WORK: Apologize and clean up as fast as you can. Also, check other rooms, not just the one you've been in. If you've been busy, your little darling may have decided to do some solo exploration. Finding a "gift" in the boardroom or at the CEO's desk will not bode well for your career. Always bring along paper towels, stain remover, and a cleaner that breaks down enzymes so that no other dog will believe the spot is the designated bathroom area.

 WHAT NOT TO DO: If you know your dog may not be reliable indoors in a strange environment, do yourself a favor and don't take him in the first place. Not only does it make it worse for the next person who wants to bring a dog to work, but if your boss is fastidious, you might find yourself on the unemployment line.

Dogs at Weddings

It's surprising how many people opt to have their dog as their best man or flower girl or simply in attendance at their wedding. Dogs are so much a part of the family. If your dog is well-behaved and the facility allows it, there's no reason not to allow the four-legged family member to participate, although this idea would seem to work best at outdoor events. Places where food is served don't allow dogs indoors unless they're Service or Therapy dogs who meet standards and regulations and have the paperwork or work jacket to prove it.

Only Four Stars for Fido: Restaurants and Hotels

U.S. restaurants are getting better about allowing dogs to dine outside with their owners, unlike most of Europe's restaurants, where dogs are not only welcome but also catered to. Frankly, I find most dogs better behaved than a lot of children I see in restaurants and coffee shops. There's no reason that both species shouldn't be well-mannered in public.

Usually, you can bring along a portable water dish (folding ones are available), and your dog can sit or lie quietly near you while you dine outdoors at dog-friendly restaurants. You can bring a treat with you for your dog, perhaps little pieces of kibble from his regular diet or a small biscuit that you can break in pieces and reward him with when he sits or lies down nicely.

More and more hotels are noticing that people want to travel with their pets, and they have created special programs for pets, with designer dog beds and gift baskets. Some restaurants will even whip up something special in the kitchen! Many motel chains also welcome pets. Most hotels and motels, however, will require a deposit on your credit card against possible damage to the room. If you allow your dog to damage the room, you will ruin this privilege for every other dog owner, so please remember that every time you take your dog out, he's an ambassador for canines. Don't leave hotels rooms dirty or trashed, because every time an irresponsible owner does that, it ruins the possibility for the responsible owners. When you check out, your hotel room shouldn't look like the morning after a frat party.

When you check in, ask the hotel to refer you to a local veterinarian, if you didn't locate one before you left home. Emergencies can happen.

Don't leave your dog alone in a hotel room for very long, if at all. If you have to leave him, be sure the television or radio is on to keep him company and give him chew toys so that he won't chew something in the room that belongs to the hotel. And be sure he's not scratching on the door trying to get out. If you leave him in the room for a brief period, you can put him in his crate with some nice toys and fresh water. Put the Do Not Disturb Sign on the door so the housekeeping staff won't frighten him. Be sure to walk him as soon as you return and remember that the crate is a tool, not punishment, so don't leave him in there with the door closed for very long. Think of your fellow travelers. No one likes a noisy person in the next room; a barking dog is even more of a nuisance to most people.

Be sure to give your dog proper exercise while traveling. Whenever you go out, whether to a hotel or restaurant, or just for a walk, take along a resealable plastic bag so that you can pick up and remove the poop. Turn the bag inside out to pick up the poop, as you turn it back, the poop will be on the inside; you can seal the bag and throw it into the proper trash receptacle.

Dog Parks

Dog parks are an interesting issue: people either love them or hate them. They are only as good as their setup, the way they're maintained, and the people who use them. No one with an aggressive dog should bring a dog to the dog park. Also, a dog park is not for children; it's for dogs, so children should not be allowed inside. Don't bring toys or treats, because other dogs may want some and start fighting. Before you bring your dog to a dog park, visit the park alone at various times of the day. See what size dogs are there, how their owners are supervising their dogs (if they're supervising their dogs!), and how the dogs are getting along. Different people and dogs will show up at different times. Is there enough room for the dogs to run?

If you have a very large dog, you don't want him accidentally injuring a very small dog during play. Some big dogs are very gentle with little dogs, but you want to be sure everyone is safe. If there isn't enough room or if people aren't being responsible, don't take your dog to that park. You are responsible for your dog's safety and well-being.

Nursing Homes and Hospitals

Therapy dogs, or dogs who visit nursing homes and hospitals, should have a suitable temperament. It will help if your dog has passed the AKC's Canine Good Citizen (CGC) test (visit www.akc.org). Both purebreds and mixed breeds can take this test. You will probably want to be part of a local or national group like the Delta Society or Therapy Dogs International for therapy dog visits. These organizations will evaluate your dog for his suitability as a therapy dog, inform you of what's involved, and train you and your dog for these visits. For example, your dog will need to be accustomed to people using walkers, canes, and wheelchairs. And, of course, your dog will have to be current on all vaccinations.

This volunteer work for you and your dog is very rewarding, both for you and for the patient at the hospital or nursing home. Be prepared to go every week, which is a substantial commitment of time and love. You have to go weekly, because the people you visit will be counting on seeing you and your dog on a regular basis. Often, for the elderly, this is the only special attention they receive.

People who haven't spoken in years have been known to speak when a dog is brought into the room. Or they will begin speaking with others in the common room because the discussion begins to revolve around the dog, and then moves to the dogs they've had in their lives.

Dogs can also help with physical therapy. Brushing a

dog is a good hand-and-arm coordination exercise for someone who has been refusing to do his or her physical therapy. Throwing a ball for the dog to retrieve can also aid in physical therapy. Dogs can do amazing things just with their presence and their sensitivity to humans. You and your dog will find this very rewarding if you're both suited to therapy visits. You want to be sure that your dog has a suitable temperament, and be sure to watch him for signs of stress. Do some exercises to help him destress, perhaps some massage. Take him home early if you begin to see signs of stress such as yawning, lip-licking, eye-blinking, or head-turning.

CONCLUSION
Putting These Behaviors to Work for Life

BEING A DOG OWNER MEANS REAPING
amazing rewards of love and companionship, but it also
requires something in exchange: commitment. You have to
be willing to commit yourself to being a responsible owner,
not just limiting that to feeding and exercising your dog and
making sure she has good veterinary care but also to training and being sure that you are both good citizens. It means
preventing problems before they start, seeking positive
assistance from qualified professionals to deal with existing
problems, and knowing that whatever you do not only
reflects on you and your dog but on other dogs and owners, too. It also means having fun with your dog and making life fun and interesting for her.

The love you pour into her will be returned multiplied.
There is nothing quite like the human-animal bond.
Cherish it and appreciate it for what it is: very special.

I hope you've learned a thing or two and know that you are not alone in any problems you face. Will your dog be a perfect canine citizen from here on out? Of course not. But, as the following story shows, sometimes the behavior that is most annoying is what we remember most . . . if only we can lighten up about it.

Memories Are Made of This . . .

"My Mira Deara was famous for her coverups. Given a correction, at least from a distance, Mira would persist in doing what she wanted until she thought you really meant business. Having followed the same approach myself most of my life, I could appreciate that.

One evening, I sat on the sofa reading a magazine when I heard the sound of dog teeth on plastic. I looked up to see puppy Mira walking into the living room with the empty container that once held that evening's chicken. I thought of Oliver Twist and his plea, 'Please sir . . . I'd like some more!' as she stood there, with the container held upright, and looked at me.

Mira then lay down and began chewing on that plastic container. 'Gnak, gnak, gnak!' I told her to stop, and she ignored me. I repeated it, using her name. Same thing. I tried enticing her with a doggie chew I had near me on the couch. Nope. I was talking to the wall.

When I got up to remove the container from her mouth, Mira lay her head on the floor and pretended to sleep. I was astonished. Before I could say anything, she cracked open one eye and saw me still standing there, my hands on my hips. She promptly closed that eye again and 'slept' some more.

I smiled, and then laughed to myself at this puppy girl's clever approach to being caught in a mischievous act. Mira, for her part, cracked open her eye one more time and upon seeing me smile, kept her head down and eyes closed but her tail thumped on the floor. When she heard me laugh out loud (the tail thumping did it), she opened both eyes, lifted her head, and clearly knew she was forgiven.

That was the first of the 'I was sleeping' excuses Mira gave me in her life. There were so many times I'd go to find out what a noise was or to see who was behind a pile of shredded paper or trail of bathroom tissue. There she would be, eyes closed, innocently dreaming . . . or so she pretended.

Mira died recently from pancreatitis brought about by her chemo treatment for lymphoma. I'd have given anything to see her thump her tail and crack open an eye to look at me that last time I saw her 'sleeping' at the emergency clinic. For now, it's memories like Mira and her chicken container that make me smile, and while I still get teary thinking of her, I wouldn't give up a minute of my life with that girl. She was a treasure and I am rich for having her with me the five and a half years we shared. " —Pauline

 As this vignette illustrates, enjoy your dog and all of her little "quirks" while you can.

RESOURCES

HERE, YOU'LL FIND SUGGESTED books, as well as DVDs and websites that may be of interest. I suggest that you never stop learning. The more you know, the more there is to know, and the better you can help your dog. It's preferable to prevent problems before they begin. And always remember the human-animal bond; the more you do with your dog, the better the bond, and the more it strengthens.

Books

Arden, Darlene. *The Angell Memorial Animal Hospital Book of Wellness and Preventive Care for Dogs.* New York: McGraw-Hill, 2002.

Arden, Darlene. *Small Dogs, Big Hearts.* Hoboken, NJ: John Wiley & Sons Publishing, 2006.

Arden, Darlene. *Unbelievably Good Deals and Great Adventures That You Absolutely Can't Get Unless You're a Dog.* New York: McGraw-Hill, 2004.

Book, Mandy, and Cheryl S. Smith. *Right on Target! Taking Dog Training to a New Level.* Wenatchee, WA: Dogwise Publishing, 2005.

Book, Mandy, and Cheryl S. Smith. *Quick Clicks.* Carlsborg, WA: Hanalei Pets, 2001.

Nelson, Leslie. *Really Reliable Recall Booklet.* Manchester, CT: Tails-U-Win, 2002.

Parsons, Emma. *Click to Calm: Healing the Aggressive Dog.* Waltham, MA: Sunshine Books, 2004.

Pryor, Karen. *Clicker Training for Dogs.* Waltham, MA: Sunshine Books, 2001.

Pryor. Karen. *Don't Shoot the Dog: The New Art of Teaching and Training.* New York: Bantam Books, 1999.

Rugaas, Turid. *On Talking Terms with Dogs: Calming Signals.* Wenatchee, WA: Dogwise Publishing, 2006.

Ryan, Terry. *The Bark Stops Here.* Sequim, WA: Legacy Canine Behavior & Training, 2000.

Smith, Cheryl S. *The Rosetta Bone.* Hoboken, NJ: Howell Book House, 2004.

Spector, Morgan. *Clicker Training for Obedience.* Waltham, MA: Sunshine Books, 1998.

DVDs and Videos

Broitman, Virginia, and Sherri Lippman. *The How of Bow Wow: Building, Proofing and Polishing Behaviors*. Ashland, VA: Take a Bow Wow, 2003.

Rugaas, Turid. *Calming Signals: What Your Dog Tells You*. Wenatchee, WA: Dogwise Publishing, 2005.

Websites

You'll find websites covering tens of thousands of dog topics. The following are my favorites.

Behavior

www.davbc.org: This is the website of the American College of Veterinary Behaviorists, the board-certified veterinarians who specialize in behavior.

www.appliedanimalbehavior.org: This organization is for Ph.D. behaviorists, although some board-certified veterinary behaviorists are also members.

www.iaabc.org: The International Association of Animal Behavior Consultants has certified behavior consultants. There are veterinarians, Ph.D. behaviorists, speakers, and trainers who have worked to receive certification from this organization and must earn continuing education units to maintain certification as well as to earn certification.

Training

Note: As with anything you do with and for your dog, be sure to visit a class without your dog to see whether the training method is truly positive. Also watch for the reactions of the dogs and their owners. If they appear anxious and/or the dogs appear frightened, go somewhere else.

www.apdt.org: The Association of Pet Dog Trainers offers a listing of dog trainers by state.

www.clickertraining.com: Karen Pryor and Sunshine Books site have everything you need to know about clicker training and a vast array of books, videos, DVDs, and so on. Take time to explore. There is also a listing of clicker trainers by state and country.

Having Fun with Your Dog

www.dogscouts.com: Yep, Dog Scouts of America. You and your dog can share the scouting experience while your dog earns merit badges just like any other good scout! They have camps and outings.

www.worldcaninefreestyle.org: The sport of Canine Musical Freestyle is a choreographed dance routine to music with your dog. It can be done by any dog of any size, age, whether purebred or mixed-breed. You can also join the discussion list on the website.

INDEX

Terms in italics indicate training behaviors.

ABOUT THE AUTHOR

DARLENE ARDEN is the author of *Unbelievably Good Deals and Great Adventures That You Absolutely Can't Get Unless You're a Dog; The Angell Memorial Animal Hospital Book of Wellness and Preventive Care for Dogs; The Irrepressible Toy Dog;* and *Small Dogs, Big Hearts.* Darlene specializes in behavior issues of dogs twenty pounds and under, but of course she is certified to deal with behavior issues of dogs of all sizes. She also teaches part of a course for dog trainers at Kutztown University, Kutztown, PA. Visit her website at www.darlenearden.com.

YOU'VE GOT QUESTIONS?